HOW TO GIVE
Effective
Feedback
TO YOUR STUDENTS

SECOND EDITION

Other books by Author

SUSAN M.
BROOKHART

HOW TO GIVE
Effective
Feedback
TO YOUR STUDENTS

SECOND EDITION

ASCD

1703 N. Beauregard St. • Alexandria, VA 22311-1714 USA
Phone: 800-933-2723 or 703-578-9600 • Fax: 703-575-5400
Website: www.ascd.org • E-mail: member@ascd.org
Author guidelines: www.ascd.org/write

Deborah S. Delisle, *Executive Director;* Robert D. Clouse, *Managing Director, Digital Content & Publications;* Stefani Roth, *Publisher;* Genny Ostertag, *Director, Content Acquisitions;* Allison Scott, *Acquisitions Editor;* Julie Houtz, *Director, Book Editing & Production;* Joy Scott Ressler, *Editor;* Melissa Johnston, *Senior Graphic Designer;* Mike Kalyan, *Director, Production Services;* Cynthia Stock, *Production Designer;* Kyle Steichen, *Senior Production Specialist*

PAPERBACK ISBN: 978-1-4166-2306-9   ASCD product #116066 n2/17
PDF E-BOOK ISBN: 978-1-4166-2309-0; see Books in Print for other formats.

Quantity discounts are available: e-mail programteam@ascd.org or call 800-933-2723, ext. 5773, or 703-575-5773. For desk copies, go to www.ascd.org/deskcopy.

Library of Congress Cataloging-in-Publication Data

Names: Brookhart, Susan M., author.
Title: How to give effective feedback to your students / Susan M. Brookhart.
Description: Second edition. | Alexandria, Virginia : ASCD, [2017] | Includes
    bibliographical references and index.
Identifiers: LCCN 2016045329 (print) | LCCN 2016057436 (ebook) | ISBN
    9781416623069 (pbk.) | ISBN 9781416623090 (EPUB)
Subjects: LCSH: Teacher-student relationships. | Communication in education.
    | Feedback (Psychology)
Classification: LCC LB1033 .B658 2017 (print) | LCC LB1033 (ebook) | DDC
    371.102/3–dc23

LC record available at https://lccn.loc.gov/2016045329

23 22 21   4 5 6 7 8 9 10 11 12

HOW TO GIVE Effective Feedback TO YOUR STUDENTS

SECOND EDITION

Feedback: An Overview

Feedback says to a student, "Somebody cared enough about my work to read it and think about it!" Most teachers want to be that "somebody." Feedback matches specific descriptions and suggestions with a particular student's work. It is just-in-time, just-for-me information delivered when and where it can do the most good.

This book is intended to help teachers provide such feedback to students. The focus is on feedback that comes from a teacher to a student and is based on student work. In the context of the book, the term *feedback* means "teacher feedback on student schoolwork." Important as they are, responses to student behavior are not considered here.

Feedback as Part of Formative Assessment

Feedback is an important component of the formative assessment process. Formative assessment gives information to teachers *and students* about how students are doing relative to classroom learning goals. From the student's point of view, the formative assessment "script" reads like this: "What knowledge or skills do I aim to develop? How close am I now? What do I need to do next?" Giving good feedback is one of the skills teachers need to master as part of good formative assessment. Other formative assessment skills include having clear learning targets, crafting clear lessons and assignments that communicate those targets to students, and—usually after giving good feedback—helping students learn how to formulate new goals for themselves and action plans that will lead to achievement of those goals.

Feedback can be very powerful if done well. The power of formative feedback lies in its double-barreled approach, addressing both cognitive and motivational factors at the same time. Good feedback gives students information they need so they can understand where they are in their learning and what to do next—the cognitive factor. Once they feel they understand what to do and why, most students develop a feeling that they have control over their own learning—the motivational factor.

Good feedback contains information that students can use, which means that students have to be able to hear and understand it. Students can't hear something that's beyond their comprehension; nor can they hear something if they are not listening or feel like it would be useless to listen. Because students' feelings of control and self-efficacy are involved, even well-intentioned feedback can be very destructive ("See? I knew I was stupid!"). The research on feedback shows its Jekyll-and-Hyde character. Not all studies about feedback show positive effects. The nature of the feedback and the context in which it is given matter a great deal.

Feedback as Part of the Formative Learning Cycle

This second edition of *How to Give Effective Feedback to Your Students* is expanded from the first edition in several ways, all of which have to do with placing feedback in the context of the formative learning cycle. In the years since the first edition, I have come to realize more deeply the role of feedback in the regulation of learning and the formative learning cycle (Andrade & Brookhart, in press; Moss & Brookhart, 2015). We will explore these ideas further in future chapters. For now, the important point is that feedback should be part of a learning process. Even the most elegantly phrased feedback message will not improve learning unless both the teacher and student learn from the feedback process and unless the student has, and takes advantage of, an opportunity to use the feedback. This second edition adds information about both of those parts of the process and therefore presents a more complete picture of feedback in the context of classroom learning.

Briefly, you can think of the formative learning cycle as the structure within a lesson that allows students to experience the three formative assessment questions (Hattie & Timperley, 2007; Sadler, 1989): Where am I going? Where am I now? and How do I close the gap? (sometimes written "Where to next?"). The most effective learning occurs when students know what it is they are trying to learn, use criteria to actively compare their current work to the goal, and take action to improve (Moss & Brookhart, 2012). Formative feedback is part of this process. It is not giving comments on final work at the end of the lesson. There is no ongoing learning process there; the work either goes home or gets thrown away, and the student may or may not remember the comments the next time she does similar work. Formative feedback involves giving comments (or arranging for self- or peer assessment), then giving a student additional performance opportunities within the same learning cycle. Even feedback that occurs on that additional work should feed students forward to the learning that comes next, usually the next lesson's learning target. Figure 1.1 describes this process in diagram form.

Figure 1.1   Feedback Feeds Forward: Feedback and the Formative Learning Cycle

Feedback (dotted lines) helps students improve learning within each lesson's formative learning cycle and from one lesson to the next.

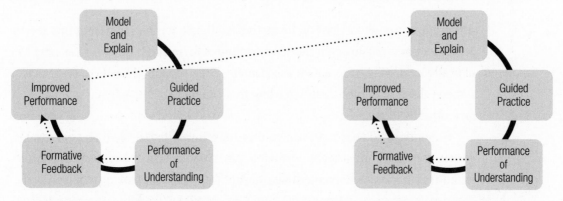

Source: Adapted from *Learning Targets: Helping Students Aim for Understanding in Today's Lesson* (p. 22), by C. M. Moss and S. M. Brookhart, 2012, Alexandria, VA: ASCD. Copyright 2012 by ASCD.

The "Three Lenses"

This book will use the metaphor of "three lenses"—a microscope lens, a camera lens, and a telescope lens—to describe how to give effective feedback that students can use in the formative learning cycle. In the years since the first edition, I have done a lot of professional development on the topic of feedback, and I have found that thinking in terms of these three lenses is helpful. The "micro view" means looking at the feedback message itself, as if through a microscope, analyzing what is said or written and how the message is delivered. The "snapshot view" means looking at the feedback as an episode of learning, as if a camera were taking a snapshot of the learning. In the snapshot view, we ask two questions: What did the teacher learn from the feedback episode, and what did the student learn from it? The "long view" means looking at the results of the feedback, as if looking through a telescope into the distance. Did students have an opportunity to use the feedback, did that in fact occur, and did learning improve?

Figure 1.2 presents a Feedback Analysis Guide that I often use to help teachers focus on the three lenses and to emphasize that the quality of feedback rests on synthesizing what's learned from the three perspectives, not just the feedback message itself.

Feedback and Grading

Although this book focuses on formative feedback, it is worth noting that feedback has traditionally occurred (and continues to, in some quarters) as part of grading—that is, summative assessment. This section gives an overview of issues related to feedback and grading that I hope will help explain my focus on formative feedback.

Going back 50 years, several studies have investigated the effects of grades versus comments on student performance. In one classic study, Page (1958) found that student achievement was higher for a group receiving prespecified comments instead of letter grades and higher still for students receiving free comments written by the teacher. Writing comments was more effective for

Figure 1.2   Feedback Analysis Guide

Micro view

Evaluate the feedback.

- Is it descriptive?
- Is it timely?
- Does it contain the right amount of information?
- Does it compare the work to criteria?
- Does it focus on the work?
- Does it focus on the process?
- Is it positive?
- Is it clear (to the student)?
- Is it specific (but not too specific)?
- Does its tone imply the student is an active learner?

Snapshot view

What evidence of learning does the feedback provide?

What did the student learn from it?

What did the teacher learn from it?

Long view

What next step(s) should the teacher and student take to use this feedback for learning? How were these steps taken? Did learning improve?

learning than giving grades. Other researchers have replicated Page's study many times over the years, with some replicating the results and others not (Stewart & White, 1976). More recent research has identified the problem: in the earliest studies, the "feedback" provided was evaluative or judgmental rather than descriptive. Page himself described the prespecified comments as words that were "thought to be 'encouraging'" (1958, p. 180). Evaluative feedback is not always helpful.

The nature of "comment studies" changed as the literature on motivation began to point to the importance of the functional significance of feedback— that is, whether the student *experiences* the comment as information or as judgment. Butler and Nisan (1986) investigated the effects of grades (evaluative), comments (descriptive), or no feedback on both learning and motivation. They used two different tasks—one quantitative task and one divergent-thinking task. Students who received descriptive comments as feedback on their first session's work performed better on both tasks in the final session and reported feeling more motivated about their work. Students who received evaluative grades as feedback on their first session's work performed well on the quantitative task in the final session but poorly on the divergent-thinking task and were less motivated. The students who received no feedback performed poorly on both tasks in the final session and also were less motivated.

Butler and Nisan's experiment illustrates several of the aspects of feedback discussed in this book. First, the comments that were successful were about the task. Second, they were descriptive. Third, they affected both performance and motivation, thus demonstrating what I call the "double-barreled" effect of formative feedback. And fourth, they fostered interest in the learning for its own sake, an orientation found in successful, self-regulated learners. Butler and Nisan's work affirms an observation that many classroom teachers have made about their students: if a paper is returned with both a grade and a comment, many students will pay attention to the grade and ignore the comment. The grade "trumps" the comment; the student will read a comment that the teacher intended to be descriptive as an explanation of the grade. Descriptive comments have the best chance of being *read* as descriptive if they are not accompanied by a grade.

Looking Ahead

This book is organized according to the three lenses described earlier. For each lens, I present some relevant research and then describe how to apply the lessons of the research in practice.

Chapters 2, 3, and 4 are about the content of the feedback message itself—the "micro view." Conclusions drawn from literature reviews on studies of feedback inform the practical checklist in the upper left portion of Figure 1.2.

Chapter 5 is about viewing feedback as an episode of learning—the "snapshot view"—and cites literature from some current studies of formative assessment. What is emerging from this literature—which admittedly is still in its infancy—is that teachers who respond to *what students are thinking* are more effective at formative assessment than those who respond to *how many correct answers* students get. This finding has huge implications for feedback. In Chapter 5, I suggest ways to look at student work for evidence of student thinking and how to connect that to feedback messages about where students are and what they should do next. The upper right portion of Figure 1.2 reminds us to analyze feedback episodes by describing what both the teacher and the student learned. Teachers should learn how students are thinking about the learning target or goal they are pursuing. Students, of course, should learn where they are in their learning and what to do next.

Chapter 6 is about helping students use feedback—the "long view"—and cites reviews of studies of the regulation of learning and studies of self- and peer assessment. Practical implications of the findings from these studies for instructional planning include arranging activities where students analyze and use their feedback, alone or with peers, and produce evidence that the feedback resulted in learning. To close the loop, teachers can give students feedback on that very point, making sure they know that their thoughtful use of feedback led to better work—giving what Hattie and Timperley (2007) would call feedback about the processing of the task and about self-regulation. The lower panel (the "long view" portion) of Figure 1.2 reminds us to build opportunities for students to use feedback into instructional planning, and to check that learning does in fact occur.

Finally, Chapters 7 and 8 address two important topics that cut across the three lenses. Principles of effective feedback apply to both simple and complex assignments and to all subjects and grade levels. Effective feedback takes into account both *what* the student was supposed to be learning and *who* the learner is. Chapter 7 gives more examples of feedback in English language arts and mathematics at different grade levels, to broaden the example pool and help readers transfer principles of effective feedback to their own teaching context. Chapter 8 discusses differentiating feedback for learners.

Feedback:
The Micro View—Characteristics
of the Feedback Message

Effective feedback is part of a classroom assessment environment in which students see constructive criticism as a good thing and understand that learning cannot occur without practice. If part of the classroom culture is to always "get things right," then if something needs improvement, it's "wrong." If, instead, the classroom culture values finding and using suggestions for improvement, students will be able to use feedback, plan and execute steps for improvement, and, in the long run, reach further than they could if they were stuck with assignments on which they could already get an *A* without any new learning. It is not fair to students to present them with feedback but no opportunities to use it. Nor is it fair to present students with what seems like constructive criticism and then use it against them in a grade or final evaluation.

What the Research Shows

The first studies and theories about feedback are more than 100 years old and arose out of the psychological theory called *behaviorism* (Thorndike, 1913). According to this theory, positive feedback is considered "positive reinforcement," and negative feedback is considered "punishment." Both reinforcement and punishment affect learning; thus, feedback is theorized to be effective. The problem with this theory is that not all feedback actually is effective.

More recently, scholars have tried to tease out, from a large body of research on feedback that has accumulated over the intervening 100 years, what makes some feedback effective and some ineffective (Bangert-Drowns, Kulik, Kulik, & Morgan, 1991; Butler & Winne, 1995; Hattie & Timperley, 2007; Kluger & DeNisi, 1996; Shute, 2008; Van der Kleij, Feskens, & Eggen, 2015). Other researchers have concentrated on describing the characteristics of effective feedback (Johnston, 2004; Tunstall & Gipps, 1996).

Educational theorists no longer explain learning with behaviorist theories about stimulus-response connections. More recent studies recognize the role of students in the feedback process. They study the kind of feedback given and the context in which it is presented. What we now realize is that the message sent is filtered through the student's perception (influenced by prior knowledge, experiences, and motivation) as it becomes the message received. The student's job is to make meaning from schoolwork, not to respond to stimuli.

Making meaning requires using and controlling one's own thought processes. This is called *self-regulation*. Butler and Winne's (1995) research review showed that both external feedback (such as teacher feedback) and internal feedback (such as student self-evaluation) affect student knowledge and beliefs. Together they help students with self-regulation: deciding on their next learning goals, devising tactics and strategies to reach them, and producing work. An important point here is that teacher feedback is not teacher regulation. Teachers can't "make" students focus on or learn something. Rather, teacher feedback is input that, together with students' own internal input, will help the students decide where they are in regard to the learning goals they need or want to meet and what they will tackle next.

Kluger and DeNisi (1996) conducted a meta-analysis of studies of feedback and found that the average effect of feedback intervention on performance was .41. This means that across all the studies, groups receiving feedback outperformed their respective control groups by an average of .41 standard deviations—the equivalent of moving from the 50th to the 66th percentile on a standardized test. However, more than 38 percent of the effect sizes from the various studies that went into this .41 average were negative—that is, showed that control groups outperformed feedback groups. The effects of feedback depend on the nature of the feedback.

Hattie and Timperley (2007) reviewed the aforementioned studies among other works to synthesize a model of feedback that focuses on its meaning. Their review used the lens of formative assessment questions—Where am I going? How am I going? Where to next?—which they call "feedback questions." In so doing, they recognized the importance of feedback in the formative process. Feedback can be the information that drives the process, or it can be a stumbling block that derails the process.

Hattie and Timperley propose a model of feedback that distinguishes four categories:

1. Feedback about the task (such as about whether answers are right or wrong or directions to get more information),
2. Feedback about the processing of the task (such as about strategies used or strategies that could be used),
3. Feedback about self-regulation (such as about student self-evaluation or self-confidence), and
4. Feedback about the student as a person (such as pronouncements that a student is "good" or "smart").

The focus of the feedback influences its effectiveness. Feedback about the qualities of the work and the process or strategies used to do the work are most helpful. Feedback that draws students' attention to their self-regulation strategies or their abilities as learners can be effective if students hear it in a way that makes them realize they will get the results they want if they expend effort and attention. Personal comments ("Good girl!") do not draw students' attention to their learning.

Shute (2008) published a review of the feedback literature, focusing on formative feedback, just after the first edition of this book went to press. In her extensive review, she discussed many of the same issues (for example, timing, specificity, and the formative purpose of feedback) as the ones in this book and made very similar recommendations (Shute, 2008, pp. 177–180). She called for feedback focused on the task, not the learner; feedback that is specific and clear; and feedback that helps the learner focus on learning, not performance. She called for avoiding comparisons with other students and for using grades with feedback, as well as for providing immediate feedback tasks requiring procedural and conceptual knowledge and delayed feedback to promote transfer of learning. She also drew some conclusions about adjusting feedback for different learners, which we will take up in Chapter 8.

Finally, several reviews have investigated what kind of feedback enhances learning best in the context of computer-based learning (Mason & Bruning, 2001; Van der Kleij, Feskens, & Eggen, 2015). A central finding in this research is that elaborated feedback—feedback that concentrates on evidence of what students were thinking and not merely about whether their answers were correct—leads to more improvement in learning than simple knowledge of results. This finding is evident across studies of feedback in other settings, as well (Hattie & Timperley, 2007; Mason & Bruning, 2001; Shute, 2008). It also matches what is known about effective formative assessment (see Chapter 5): Feedback needs to describe where students are in relation to the learning they are aiming for and make at least one suggestion for a next step in learning.

Feedback Strategies and Content

Taken together, the major reviews discussed here have much to say about how you, the teacher, can give effective feedback. Figure 2.1 summarizes the strategic choices for feedback and makes recommendations for each based on the research. Notice that the suggestions depend on context: the characteristics of your students, the assignment, and the classroom atmosphere. There is no magic bullet that will be just the right thing for all students, all the time.

When you are deciding on a feedback strategy, you are also, of course, deciding *what* it is that you want to say to the student. Figure 2.2 summarizes the kinds of choices you have about the content of your feedback and makes recommendations based on the research.

Figure 2.1 Feedback Strategies

Feedback Strategies Can Vary in . . .	In These Ways . . .	Recommendations for Good Feedback
Timing	• When given • How often	• Provide immediate feedback for knowledge of facts (right/wrong). • Delay feedback slightly for more comprehensive reviews of student thinking and processing. • Never delay feedback beyond when it would make a difference to students. • Provide feedback as often as is practical for all major assignments.
Amount	• How many points made • How much about each point	• Prioritize—pick the most important points. • Choose points that relate to major learning goals. • Consider the student's developmental level.
Mode	• Oral • Written • Visual/demonstration	• Select the best mode for the message. Would a comment when passing the student's desk suffice? Is a conference needed? • Interactive feedback (talking with the student) is best when possible. • Give written feedback on written work or on assignment cover sheets. • Use demonstration if "how to do something" is an issue or if the student needs an example.
Audience	• Individual • Group/class	• Individual feedback sends the message, "The teacher values my learning." • Group/class feedback works if most of the class missed the same concept on an assignment, which presents an opportunity for reteaching.

Next we illustrate the different types of feedback with classroom examples of good and bad practices for each, with the exception of clarity, specificity, and tone. These "word choice" options are addressed in Chapter 3, which is specifically about the language you choose for feedback. Keep in mind that the analysis here focuses on the "micro" view of feedback—characteristics of the feedback message itself.

Figure 2.2 Feedback Content

Feedback Content Can Vary in . . .	In These Ways . . .	Recommendations for Good Feedback
Focus	• On the work itself • On the process the student used to do the work • On the student's self-regulation • On the student personally	• When possible, describe both the work and the process—and their relationship. • Comment on the student's self-regulation if the comment will foster self-efficacy. • Avoid personal comments.
Comparison	• To criteria for good work (criterion-referenced) • To other students (norm-referenced) • To student's own past performance (self-referenced)	• Use criterion-referenced feedback for giving information about the work itself. • Use norm-referenced feedback for giving information about student processes or effort. • Use self-referenced feedback for unsuccessful learners who need to see the progress they are making, not how far they are from the goal.
Function	• Description • Evaluation/judgment	• Describe. • Don't judge.
Valence	• Positive • Negative	• Use positive comments that describe what is well done. • Accompany negative descriptions of the work with positive suggestions for improvement.
Clarity	• Clear to the student • Unclear	• Use vocabulary and concepts the student will understand. • Tailor the amount and content of feedback to the student's developmental level.
Specificity	• Nitpicky • Just right • Overly general	• Tailor the degree of specificity to the student and the task. • Make feedback specific enough so that students know what to do but not so specific that it's done for them. • Identify errors or types of errors, but avoid correcting every one (e.g., copyediting or supplying right answers), which doesn't leave students anything to do.
Tone	• Implications • What the student will "hear"	• Choose words that communicate respect for the student and the work. • Choose words that position the students as the agents. • Choose words that cause students to think or wonder.

Choosing Feedback Strategies

Feedback strategies can vary in terms of timing, amount, mode, and audience. Let's examine each of these elements in turn.

Timing

The purpose of giving immediate or only slightly delayed feedback is to help students hear it and use it. Students need to receive feedback while they are still mindful of the topic, assignment, or performance in question and while they still think of the learning goal as a learning goal—that is, as something they are still striving to achieve. In fact, they *especially* need to receive feedback while they still have some reason to work on the learning goal. Feedback about a topic they won't have to deal with again all year will strike students as pointless. A general principle for gauging the timing of feedback is to put yourself in the students' place. When would students want to hear your feedback? When they are still thinking about the work, of course, and can still do something about it.

Figure 2.3 summarizes some examples of good and bad timing of feedback. The following paragraphs elaborate on one example.

Good timing: Returning tests and assignments promptly. A teacher gave a multiple-choice test, scored it later that day, and returned it to students the

Figure 2.3 Feedback Timing

Purpose: • For students to get feedback while they are still mindful of the learning target • For students to get feedback while there is still time for them to act on it	
Examples of Good Feedback Timing	**Examples of Bad Feedback Timing**
• Returning a test or assignment the next day • Giving immediate oral responses to questions of fact • Giving immediate oral responses to student misconceptions • Providing flash cards (which give immediate right/wrong feedback) for studying facts	• Returning a test or assignment two weeks after it is completed • Ignoring errors or misconceptions (thereby implying acceptance) • Going over a test or assignment when the unit is over and there is no opportunity to show improvement

next day. After she handed back the scored tests, she spent class time going over the answers. In educational psychology terms, this is called "knowledge of results." Even this simple feedback about the outcome is effective—and good to do promptly.

If you want to provide prompt feedback but feel too busy or overwhelmed to do so, consider making a special effort to catch up with feedback responsibilities. You can't be prompt with today's work if you still have last week's work on your desk. Once you are caught up, you may find that you're working at the same pace but dealing with more recent work.

Bad timing: Delaying the return of tests and assignments. We can all remember those times in school when we thought, "Is she *ever* going to return that report?" I encourage you to recall those incidents and the accompanying feelings of frustration and of being ignored to spur yourself to return your students' work promptly. This should be your regular practice, and students should know it and be able to count on it. If students do experience regular, timely feedback, they will most likely be understanding if an emergency arises and you take longer than usual to return an assignment.

Amount

Probably the hardest decision to make about feedback is deciding on the amount to provide. A natural inclination is to want to "fix" everything you see. That's the teacher's-eye view, where the target is perfect achievement of all learning goals. For real learning, what makes the difference is a usable amount of information that connects with something students already know and takes them from that point to the next level. Judging the right amount of feedback to give—how much, on how many points—requires deep knowledge and consideration of the following three factors:

- The topic in general and your learning target or targets in particular,
- Typical developmental learning progressions for those topics or targets, and
- Your individual students.

You need to consider all three factors simultaneously. Your feedback should give students a clear understanding of what to do next on a point or points that they can see they need to work on. This requires you to know your students; for some, simply getting clarity and improvement on one point is sufficient, whereas others can handle more. In order to know what *should* come next, dig into your knowledge of the topic (what else should they know?) and your teaching experience with the topic (what typically comes next?).

Try to see things from the student's-eye view. On which aspects of the learning target has the student done acceptable work? Which aspects of the learning target would the student benefit from improving upon next? Are any particular assignments coming up that would make it wiser to emphasize one point over another? Is there any particular point that you and the student have a history about? For example, if you and the student have been working hard on neatness, maybe a comment about handwriting would be right on target. If not, that comment may not be as useful as some of the other things you could say about the work. Figure 2.4 gives examples of good and bad choices about how much feedback to give, and the following paragraphs illustrate the point.

Good amount: Using the Goldilocks principle. The Goldilocks principle maintains, "Not too much, not too little, but just right." Appropriateness varies case by case, and here is just one illustration. The student work in Figure 2.5

Figure 2.4 Amount of Feedback

Purpose:
• For students to get enough feedback so that they understand what to do but not so much that the work has been done for them (differs case by case)
• For students to get feedback on "teachable moment" points but not an overwhelming number

Examples of Good Amounts of Feedback	Examples of Bad Amounts of Feedback
• Selecting two or three main points about a paper for comment	• Returning a student's paper with every error in mechanics edited
• Giving feedback on important learning targets	• Writing comments on a paper that are more voluminous than the paper itself
• Commenting on at least as many strengths as weaknesses	• Writing voluminous comments on poor-quality papers and almost nothing on good-quality papers

Figure 2.5   4th Grade "Lunchtime" Paragraph

Writing prompt: Describe what lunchtime is like for you on a school day. Be sure to tell about your lunchtime so that someone who has never had lunch with you on a school day can understand where you have lunch and what lunchtime is like.

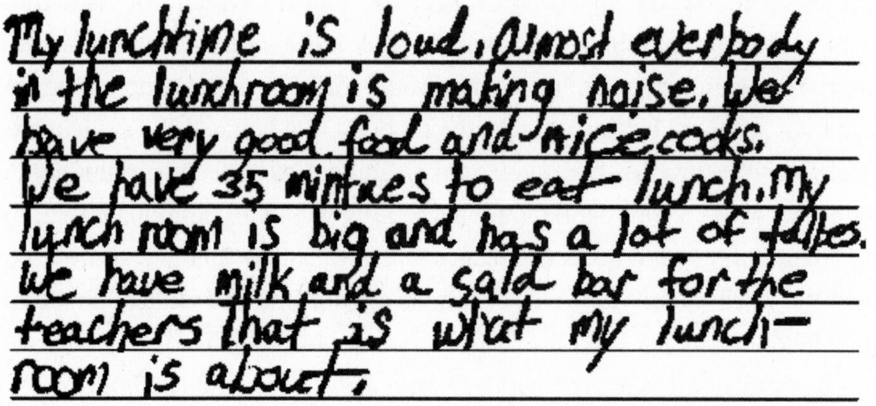

My lunchtime is loud, almost everbody in the lunchroom is making noise. We have very good food and nice cooks. We have 35 minutes to eat lunch. My lunch room is big and has a lot of talbes. We have milk and a sald bar for the teachers that is what my lunch— room is about,

Source: National Assessment of Educational Progress, sample items. Available: http://nces.ed.gov/nationsreportcard/itmrls/

is taken from the item bank for 4th grade writing of the National Assessment of Educational Progress. The task is typical of the kind of in-class assignments many students do. Suppose you were the teacher and a 4th grader had written the paragraph in Figure 2.5 for practice in class.

This paragraph is not optimal 4th grade work. However, the first and most important thing to point out is that it is clear and makes sense. This is true, and it's noteworthy. Probably the second main response to this as a piece of writing is that it is simple: it doesn't have much detail or variety in sentence structure. But if the student could think of how to add details, they would probably be included.

An initial feedback comment in this case might be: *This is clear and makes sense to me.* This comment describes the positive features of the work in relation to the learning goal: clarity and meaning in writing. The next bit of feedback might be: *More details would make this more interesting. If you move the sentence about the lunchroom being big right after "noise," you give one reason for the noise. Can you think of others? Can you describe what the noise sounds like?*

For some students, it would be advisable to stop here, with one positive comment and one suggestion for improvement. For students who are interested in further work on the goal of adding more details, the following comment would also help: *Can you give some examples of the "good food" besides milk and salad for the teachers? What kinds of food do you eat at lunch? What foods do your friends eat?* Notice that the comments not only name the criticism (that the paragraph is very simple and lacks details) but also model strategies the student might use to add details, without telling the student what those details should be. They encourage the student to think, and they imply that those next steps are within the student's repertoire of experience and understanding.

All of the above comments are probably best delivered orally because, although they are simple, they take more words to make clear than the student has written. They should also be presented at the student's desk while pointing to the relevant places in the paragraph. Once the paragraph has improved considerably, the student can proofread it for spelling and other mechanics.

Bad amount: Focusing only on mechanics. We all know teachers whose first inclination would be to use a red pen and fix the mechanics: "*Sald* should be *salad.* There should be a period after *teachers.*" This sort of thing, although important, does not advance the student as a writer as much as the comments about the writing process.

Mode

Feedback can be delivered in many modalities. Some kinds of assignments lend themselves better to written feedback (for example, reviewing and writing comments on students' written work), some to oral feedback (for example, observing and commenting as students do math problems as seatwork), and some to demonstrations (for example, helping a kindergarten student hold a pencil correctly). Some of the best feedback can result from conversations *with* the student. For example, rather than telling the student all the things you notice about his or her work, you might start by asking questions such as

"What are you noticing about this?" "Does anything surprise you?" Peter Johnston's book *Choice Words* (2004) has more discussion of how to ask questions that help students help you with feedback.

Decisions about whether to give the feedback orally or in written form should be partly based on the students' reading ability, especially for younger students. Could they understand what you would write? Such decisions are also partly based on opportunity. Talking with students is usually best, because you can have a conversation. However, you don't have the time to talk with every student about everything. Figure 2.6 presents examples of good and bad choices about the mode of presentation for feedback, and the following paragraphs provide further illustrations.

Good choice of mode: Taking advantage of a teachable moment. Recall that the feedback for the "Lunchtime" paragraph in Figure 2.5 formed the basis for a conversation with the student around two relatively simple points: the paragraph was clear, and more details were needed. These represent task-related feedback. Providing additional feedback about the process of getting details into the work would involve more words than the student wrote. Realistically, you can't write that much, and even if you did, it would have the effect, visually,

Figure 2.6   Feedback Mode

Purpose:
• To communicate the feedback message in the most appropriate way

Examples of Good Feedback Mode	Examples of Bad Feedback Mode
• Using written feedback for comments that students need to be able to save and look over • Using oral feedback for students who don't read well • Using oral feedback if there is more information to convey than students would want to read • Demonstrating how to do something if the student needs to see how to do something or what something "looks like"	• Speaking to students to save yourself the trouble of writing • Writing to students who don't read well

of overwhelming the student work. Besides, this feedback could initiate a helpful, brief conversation with the student at a teachable moment. Therefore, providing the feedback orally is a good decision.

Bad choice of mode: Writing things the student can't comprehend. Unfortunately, the following example of a bad choice is a true story. An elementary teacher assigned her class to practice handwriting by copying a story from the board. A little boy with a mild learning disability was having difficulty transferring the story he was to copy from the board onto his paper. Using a bright purple marker, the teacher made a slash on his words each time a letter was added or omitted and wrote *addition* or *omission* over it. In one place, the student wrote *og* instead of *go,* and the teacher circled it and wrote *reversal.* The little boy did not know the words *omission* and *reversal.* All he was able to conclude from the purple slashes and strange words was that the teacher thought his paper was bad. He did not understand what he had done or how he might fix it. What he learned from that feedback was that he was weighed in the balance and found wanting. If that happens too often, students give up.

Audience

The example about the bad choice of mode also provides a lesson about audience. Like all communication, feedback works best when it has a strong and appropriate sense of the audience. Feedback about the specifics of individual work is best addressed to the individual student in terms the student can understand. That simple act is powerful in itself because, in addition to the information provided, it communicates to the student a sense that you care about his or her individual progress. ("The teacher actually read and thought about what I did!") So the first point about audience is that you should know each of your students—and talk to them!

If the same message would benefit a group of students, providing feedback to the class or group can save time and also serve as a minilesson or review session. If you speak to the whole class when only a subset needs the feedback, you can use the students who have mastered the concept as the "more experienced peers," helping you demonstrate the concept or skill. Or you can pull a group aside to give some feedback while others are doing something else.

You can also mix individual and group feedback. For example, imagine you had just collected a writing assignment in which you found many students had used bland or vague terms. You might choose to give the whole class some feedback about word choice, with examples of how to use specific, precise, or vivid words instead of dull and uninteresting ones. You might couple that with some thought-provoking questions on individual students' work: "What other words could you use instead of *big*?" "How could you describe this event so someone else would see how terrible it was for you?"

Figure 2.7 presents examples of good and bad choices about the audience for feedback, and the following paragraphs elaborate the point.

Good choice of audience: Using a group approach for a math demonstration. A middle school math teacher found that about a third of the class had trouble on a homework assignment. The problem concerned drawing perpendicular bisectors. Some students were trying to measure the line segment and divide it in half instead of using a compass to draw circles around the endpoints and then connecting the points of intersection. The teacher decided that group feedback was in order, having seen the same kind of trouble on several papers.

First she told the class that she was going to go over constructing a perpendicular bisector because she had noticed that some people had had trouble with the homework and she wanted everyone to learn how to draw a perpendicular

Figure 2.7 Feedback Audience

Purpose:
• To reach the appropriate students with specific feedback
• To communicate, through feedback, that student learning is valued

Examples of Good Choice of Audience	Examples of Bad Choice of Audience
• Communicating with an individual, giving information specific to the individual performance • Giving group or class feedback when the same mini-lesson or reteaching session is required for a number of students	• Using the same comments for all students • Never giving individual feedback because it takes too much time

bisector. That comment did two things. First, it identified what she was going to do as feedback—students now knew that she was responding to their work. If the teacher had launched into the demonstration without noting that it was feedback, many students would not have made the connection. The lesson would have just been "what we're doing today." Second, the comment reminded students of the learning target, making the feedback purposeful (saying, in effect, "We have a learning target, and here's what you need to do to get closer to it").

Next, the teacher drew a line segment labeled $\overline{AB}$ on the board and asked, "What should I do first to draw a perpendicular bisector for line segment $\overline{AB}$?" She called on a student who she knew had done it successfully to come to the board and demonstrate. As he did each step, the teacher asked the class, "What is he doing now?" When that problem was done, she left it in view and drew another line segment labeled $\overline{CD}$ next to it. She called on a student who had not been successful with the homework to come to the board and demonstrate, coaching as necessary so that he completed the task successfully.

Then she passed back the homework papers. Students who had perpendicular bisector problems marked incorrect were invited to do them again (homework, after all, is for practice). By the time the chapter test rolled around, almost all the students showed that they did indeed know how to draw a perpendicular bisector.

Bad choice of audience: Math demonstration gone wrong. The scenario just described seems simple enough. But what if the teacher had found that only two of the students in the class were incorrectly measuring and then marking off half to bisect lines? The minilesson described would probably bore most of the class. Reteaching the whole class would be a bad choice of feedback audience in that case. The audience for additional feedback on bisecting lines—identifying measuring as an unproductive approach, providing reteaching and additional problems for practice—is those two students. Individual feedback would be the way to go in this case. In traditionally organized classrooms, the teacher could provide that feedback in student conferences or during seatwork. Written feedback and examples on the students' homework papers followed by further opportunities to practice in class with the teacher or with peer tutors could also be helpful. In classrooms where flexible grouping and other differentiated instruction methods are used routinely, feedback could be given in the context of small-group work on bisecting lines.

Choosing Feedback Content

Choosing the content of your feedback involves choices about focus, comparison, function, and valence. Because any feedback message embodies choices about all of these things at once, the examples address all four factors together. This section will help you decide *what* to say in your feedback. For suggestions about *how* to say things (word choices that affect the clarity, specificity, and tone of your feedback), see Chapter 5.

Focus

Hattie and Timperley (2007) distinguish four categories of feedback:

- Feedback about the task,
- Feedback about the processing of the task,
- Feedback about self-regulation, and
- Feedback about the self as a person.

Feedback about the task includes information about errors—whether something is correct or incorrect. Feedback about the task also includes information about the depth or quality of the work, often against criteria that are either explicit (for example, criteria from a scoring rubric) or implicit in the assignment (for example, a written assignment should be well written). Feedback about the task may include a need for more information (for example, "You should include more information about the First Continental Congress in this report"). Feedback about the task can also include information about neatness or format.

Feedback about the task has been found to be more powerful when it corrects misconceptions than when it alerts students to lack of information (Hattie & Timperley, 2007). If a student doesn't know something, further instruction is more powerful than feedback. One problem with feedback about the task is that it may not transfer to other tasks because it is specific to the particular assignment. In that sense, although it contributes to better learning for the task at hand, feedback about the task does not contribute to further learning as much as the second type—feedback about the process used to do the task.

Feedback about process gives students information about how they approached the task, the relationship between what they did and the quality of their performance, and possible alternative strategies that would also be useful. Some successful learners are able to translate feedback about the task into feedback about the process. That is, given *outcome feedback* (knowledge of results), they can generate their own *cognitive feedback* (linking characteristics of the task and their process with those results) (Butler & Winne, 1995).

When teachers give feedback about the process, they are effectively scaffolding this kind of transfer for all students. This is a very powerful way to address students' needs, helping them to acquire this "learning how to learn" skill. (See Chapter 6 for more about this.)

Self-regulation is the process students use to monitor and control their own learning. It can lead to students seeking, accepting, and acting on feedback information—or not. Effective learners create internal routines that include figuring out when they need more information, an assessment, or suggestions, and strategies for getting this feedback. Less effective learners depend more on external factors—such as whether the teacher decides to give any feedback on this or that assignment—for their information. Students are more willing to expend effort in getting and dealing with feedback if they have confidence in themselves as learners (that is, self-efficacy) and confidence that the information will be useful and thus worth the effort. Therefore, feedback about self-regulation is effective to the degree that it enhances self-efficacy.

Feedback about the person ("Smart girl!") is generally not a good idea, for two reasons. First, it doesn't contain information that can be used for further learning, so it's not formative. Second, and more insidious, feedback about the person can contribute to students believing that intelligence is fixed. This implies that achievement is something beyond the student's control. The belief that intelligence is fixed removes the connection between student effort and achievement (Dweck, 2007). It leads to a kind of academic fatalism. In contrast, feedback about the processes students use to do their work fosters the belief that achievement is related to specific strategies—specific kinds of effort that are under the student's control—and not to innate ability. This is not only better for learning—it's true! Figure 2.8 presents examples of good and bad choices about the focus of feedback.

Feedback about processes shows students the connections between what they did and the results they got. Simple knowledge of test results is task-related feedback. To extend it into feedback about the learning process, have students figure out the reasons for the error for each item they got wrong. This simple exercise can be done individually. Help students see that careless errors (like marking the wrong choice even though they knew the right choice) imply that being more careful and taking more time might be good strategies for improvement. Errors about facts or concepts imply that studying longer or differently might be helpful. Trying to classify what kinds of facts or concepts were particularly problematic can help students "study smarter, not harder" by focusing on the trouble spots.

Students should also be able to indicate why the right answer is correct. This activity can be done in groups and is most useful if there are more

Figure 2.8   Feedback Focus

Purpose:
• To describe specific qualities of the work in relation to the learning targets
• To make observations about students' learning processes and strategies that will help them figure out how to improve
• To foster student self-efficacy by drawing connections between students' work and their mindful, intentional efforts
• To avoid personal comments

Examples of Good Feedback Focus	Examples of Bad Feedback Focus
• Making comments about the strengths and weaknesses of a performance • Making comments about the work process you observed or recommendations about a work process or study strategy that would help improve the work • Making comments that position the student as the one who chooses to do the work • Avoiding personal comments	• Making comments that bypass the student (e.g., "This is hard" instead of "You did a good job because . . .") • Making criticisms without offering any insights into how to improve • Making personal compliments or digs (e.g., "How could you do that?" or "You idiot!")

opportunities ahead for the students to work with the material. It makes sense, in fact, to build in at least one more lesson or assignment after this kind of feedback, to provide a purpose for students' work and to send the message that it is possible, and important, to learn from mistakes. Chapter 6 includes an extended example and a form for doing this.

Comparison

You may be accustomed to thinking about norm-referencing (comparing student performance to that of other students) and criterion-referencing (comparing student performance to a standard) in relation to test scores. Feedback also uses comparisons.

Comparing student work to criteria for success on a learning goal is criterion-referencing, and it is the primary kind of comparison to use for good feedback. ("All your details support your thesis that sharks are misunderstood except this one. I don't see what it has to do with sharks.") This feedback helps the *student* decide what the next goal should be. Feedback against clear criteria matches with the model of instruction used in most classrooms. Most teachers use an instructional model that starts with a learning target (sometimes called a goal or an objective). What does the target look like? How will the students know how close they get? How close did they, in fact, get on this assignment? These are the questions that criterion-referenced feedback answers, and they are the questions students need to have answered in order to learn.

Self-referenced feedback is helpful for describing the processes or methods students use ("I see you checked your work this time. Your computations were better than last time too! See how well that works?"). Self-referenced feedback about the work itself is also helpful for struggling students who need to understand they can make progress ("Did you notice you have all the names capitalized this time? You had trouble with that last time."). Chapter 8 considers this use in more detail.

Just for the sake of completeness, I'll define norm-referenced feedback. Such feedback is not generally recommended, because it doesn't contain information the student can use to improve. Norm-referencing compares a student's performance to the performance of other students. Suppose, for example,

Trisha's paper was judged to be not as good as her neighbor's. If she had the chance to do it over, what would she do? Other than copy her neighbor's paper, she really doesn't have anything to go on. Even worse, norm-referenced feedback creates winners and losers and plays into that fatalistic mindset that says student ability, not strategic work, is what's important.

Given the competitiveness that is trained into many students in the United States, sometimes students want norm-referenced information. In the context of *summative assessment only*, not formative assessment, I have seen teachers give limited norm-referenced information as a way of helping students answer the question "How did I do?" For instance, when handing back a graded assignment, a teacher may put the grade distribution on the board (7 *A*s, 10 *B*s, and so on) so that students can see where they are. This approach can be useful in a class where you are sure all the students are successful learners. As with all feedback, understanding the context is absolutely crucial. Norm-referencing is so dangerous to the motivation of unsuccessful learners—or those who feel that way, whether they are or not—that I don't recommend it. And the research doesn't either.

Figure 2.9 presents examples of good and bad choices about the kinds of comparisons used in feedback.

Figure 2.9   Kinds of Comparisons Used in Feedback

Purpose:
• Usually, to compare student work with established criteria
• Sometimes, to compare a student's work with his or her own past performance
• Rarely, to compare a student's work with the work of other students

Examples of Good Kinds of Comparisons	Examples of Bad Kinds of Comparisons
• Comparing work to student-generated rubrics • Comparing student work to rubrics that have been shared ahead of time • Encouraging a reluctant student who has improved, even though the work is not yet good	• Putting up wall charts that compare students with one another • Giving feedback on each student's work according to different criteria or no criteria

Function

If only using "descriptive" versus "evaluative" feedback were simply a matter of wordsmithing! We could all learn how to write descriptive feedback just as we learned to write descriptive paragraphs in elementary school. Unfortunately, part of the issue is how the student understands the comment. Students filter what they hear through their own past experiences, good and bad.

Students are less likely to pay attention to descriptive feedback if it is accompanied by judgments, such as a grade or an evaluative comment. Some students will even hear "judgment" when you intended description. Some unsuccessful learners have been so frustrated by their school experiences that they might see even an attempt to help them as just another declaration that they are "stupid." For these learners, it helps to point out improvements over their own last performance, even if those improvements don't amount to success on the assignment. Then, select one or two small, doable next steps for the student; after the next round of work, give feedback on the success with those steps, and so on.

However, there are some things you can do to maximize the chances that students will interpret the feedback you give as descriptive. First, give students lots of opportunities to practice and receive feedback without a grade being involved. Some teachers find this hard to do. (Have you ever said, "Everything you do counts in my class"?) However, it doesn't make sense to have students always work on learning targets that are easy enough that they can get an *A* or a *B* the first time they try it. It will take a while, but if you work at it, you can shift what students see as "counting." If they attempt moderately challenging work, are exposed to feedback that they can see makes their work better, are allowed to practice until they improve, and *then* do a test or an assignment "for a grade," most will realize that they benefit. These student feelings of control over their work and self-regulation will dwarf any kind of "control" you engineered by grading everything. If your students need some scaffolding as they develop these kinds of work habits, you might have to work up to it. In the end, though, feedback without the opportunity to use it to improve really is pointless. Second, make your feedback observational. Describe what you see. How close is it to the learning target? What do you think would help?

Figure 2.10   Feedback Function

Purpose (for Formative Assessment):	
• To describe student work	
• To avoid evaluating or "judging" student work in a way that would stop students from trying to improve	

Examples of Good Feedback Function	Examples of Bad Feedback Function
• Identifying for students the strengths and weaknesses in the work • Expressing what you observe in the work	• Putting a grade on work intended for practice or formative purposes • Telling students the work is "good" or "bad" • Giving rewards or punishments • Giving general praise or general criticism

Figure 2.10 presents some examples of good and bad choices of descriptive and evaluative feedback.

Valence

Feedback should be positive. Being "positive" doesn't mean being artificially happy or saying work is good when it isn't. Being positive means describing how the strengths in a student's work match the criteria for good work and how those strengths show what the student is learning. Being positive means pointing out where improvement is needed and suggesting things the student could do about it. Just noticing what is wrong without offering suggestions to make it right is not helpful. Figure 2.11 presents examples of good and bad choices about the valence (positive or negative) of feedback.

Tunstall and Gipps (1996) developed a typology of teacher feedback based on observations in primary schools. They divided feedback into two main kinds: descriptive and evaluative. Positive evaluative feedback includes rewards, general praise, and the like. Negative evaluative feedback includes punishments, general criticisms, and so on. On the descriptive side, however, all of the feedback has a positive intention. Even criticism, if it is descriptive and not judgmental, is intended to be constructive. Tunstall and Gipps talk about descriptive feedback as being composed of *achievement feedback* and *improvement feedback*.

Figure 2.11 Feedback Valence

Purpose:
• To use positive comments that describe what is done well
• To make suggestions about what could be done for improvement

Examples of Good Feedback Valence	Examples of Bad Feedback Valence
• Being positive • Even when criticizing, being constructive • Making suggestions (not prescriptions or pronouncements)	• Finding fault • Describing what is wrong and offering no suggestions about what to do • Punishing or denigrating students for poor work

Achievement feedback describes or affirms for a student what was done well and why. Improvement feedback describes for a student what more could be done and what strategies might lead to improvement of the work.

Examples of the kinds of comments a teacher might make are presented in Figure 2.12, along with comments about their focus, kind of comparison, function, and valence. The comments are also listed as examples of "good feedback" and "bad feedback," but keep in mind that the context makes a difference. The examples of "bad feedback" are almost never appropriate, but without context, that's as much as we can say about the chart. Even the examples of "good feedback" wouldn't be appropriate for students who didn't need to hear them.

How to Know Whether Your Feedback Is Good

The examples in Figure 2.12 show how choices about feedback content affect the message that is sent and therefore how the student will probably respond. You can use the top left panel of the Feedback Analysis Guide (the "micro view") in Figure 1.2 (see p. 5) to check these feedback choices.

Student response is the ultimate criterion against which you can evaluate your own feedback. We'll talk more about feedback as an episode of learning (the "snapshot view") and feedback that improves learning (the "long view").

Figure 2.12   Examples of Feedback Content

Feedback	Types of Focus, Comparison, Function, and Valence
Each paragraph should have one main idea, and that idea goes in the topic sentence.	• Focus—Task • Comparison—Criterion-referenced • Function—Descriptive • Valence—Positive This is an example of **good feedback** if the student needs this information about what paragraphs should contain.
Your details strongly support your claim that we should recycle newspapers. That's great. Where did you find all those facts?	• Focus—Task, process, self-regulation • Comparison—Criterion-referenced • Function—Descriptive • Valence—Positive This is an example of **good feedback.** It confirms for the student that the work meets one of the targets (strong supporting details) and connects this success to student effort (the student did research to find out facts, and the teacher noticed).
This report probably wouldn't convince a reader who didn't already agree we should recycle. What else could you do to make a more convincing argument?	• Focus—Task, process • Comparison—Criterion-referenced • Function—Descriptive, naming weakness in terms of criteria and suggesting the student think about improvement strategies • Valence—Critical, but pointing forward This is an example of **good feedback** for a student who the teacher believes already knows what to do (look up more information in more sources). Such a response makes the student the one to decide on the regulation. It would not be good feedback if the teacher truly did not think the student knew what was missing.
This report probably wouldn't convince a reader who didn't already agree we should recycle. I would want to know more about the effects on the environment and the cost of recycling.	• Focus—Task, process • Comparison—Criterion-referenced • Function—Descriptive, naming weakness in terms of criteria and suggesting improvement strategies • Valence—Constructive criticism This is an example of **good feedback** for a student who the teacher believes does not know what is missing in his or her report. It suggests what the student could do to improve the report.

Feedback	Types of Focus, Comparison, Function, and Valence
Your report was the shortest one in the class. You didn't put enough in it.	• Focus—Task, process, personal • Comparison—Norm-referenced • Function—Judgmental • Valence—Negative This is an example of **bad feedback**. The teacher aims to communicate the same feedback message as in the previous box. Saying it this way, however, implies that the student is competing with others (as opposed to aiming for a learning target) and that the reason the work is poor is that the student "did something bad." The student ends up feeling judged and not motivated to improve.
This report is better than your last one. You've made it clear you think we should recycle newspapers. What would make it even better is more facts about what would happen if we did recycle—more about how many trees we would save, things like that.	• Focus—Task, process • Comparison—Self-referenced • Function—Descriptive • Valence—Positive, plus constructive criticism This is an example of **good feedback** that uses self-referenced comparisons in conjunction with descriptive information about the task to show struggling students that their work is making a difference. Then, when the teacher suggests what they need to do next, they may be more likely to think they can do it. Notice too that the teacher makes one suggestion (and probably also made one last time): it's important to be clear about the main point. Giving feedback about small steps helps students who would be overwhelmed by having to improve in many areas at once.
Your report is the best one in the class! You can have a "free pass" for your homework tonight.	• Focus—Personal (it says the report is great, but the attribution seems to be that this is a "good" student) • Comparison—Norm-referenced • Function—Judgmental • Valence—Positive This is an example of **bad feedback**. It does not tell the student what is good about the report. It also rewards the student by changing an unrelated assignment.

(*continued*)

Figure 2.12   Examples of Feedback Content (*Continued*)

Feedback	Types of Focus, Comparison, Function, and Valence
I love the chart that starts with trees and ends up at the recycling plant (instead of back at more trees). It follows the relevant section of your report and illustrates the complete cycle so clearly! How did you come up with that idea?	• Focus—Task, process, self-regulation • Comparison—Criterion-referenced • Function—Descriptive • Valence—Positive This is an example of **good feedback** that does what the previous example may have intended to do. It selects an unusual, positive feature of a good report, notices that this must have been an original idea, and asks the student to reflect on how he or she came up with the idea. Having the student name the strategy used will strengthen this student's self-regulation abilities and probably increase self-efficacy.
Your report is late! What's the matter with you?	• Focus—Personal • Comparison—Criterion-referenced (implied—being on time) • Function—Judgmental • Valence—Negative This is an example of **bad feedback**. Of course there is a problem if work is late. However, put yourself in the student's position. Would this comment really inspire you to finish your work and turn it in?
[Name], I don't have your report. Can you tell me what happened?	• Focus—Process • Comparison—Criterion-referenced (implied—being on time) • Function—Descriptive • Valence—Open at this point, soliciting information This is a better example than the previous one of feedback to deliver the message that work is late.

The Feedback Analysis Guide will help you evaluate those aspects of your feedback as well, after reading about them in Chapters 5 and 6. It's important, however, to foreshadow that that is where we are headed in our quest for effective feedback. Feedback that merely follows the principles in the micro view checklist, but does not lead to learning, is by definition not effective. Your feedback is effective if it gets the following results:

- Your students do learn—their work does improve.
- Your students become more motivated—they believe they can learn, they want to learn, and they take more control over their own learning.
- Your classroom becomes a place where feedback, including constructive criticism, is valued and viewed as productive.

Focus, comparison, function, and valence are choices about *what* to say in your feedback. You also have choices about *how* you say things—about clarity, specificity, and tone. Chapter 3 discusses these types of choices.

3

Feedback:
The Micro View—Written Feedback

Written feedback is a genre all its own. Word choice matters. Tone matters. For example, consider these two comments written in the margin of a student essay: "You aren't clear here" and "I don't see what you mean here." Both intend to convey the same thing, but the first sounds more judgmental and the second, more descriptive. This chapter gives tips and strategies for clearly communicating the intended messages. It also discusses deciding on the method to use for giving written feedback—for example, writing comments directly on student work or making notes on a rubric or an assignment cover sheet.

Writing good feedback requires an understanding that language does more than describe our world; it helps us construct our world. Consider the worldview implicit in this comment: "What did you think about when you chose that topic? What were you trying to accomplish?" It implies the student is someone who thinks and that the choice the student made had purpose. It invites the student to discuss the choice and presumably go on to discuss whether the paper can accomplish what was intended. It positions the student as the chooser and as someone who can have a conversation with the teacher.

Now consider the worldview implicit in this comment: "You won't find much about carrier pigeons. That's too narrow a topic. Pick something else." This comment positions the student as passive (a taker of orders from the teacher) and the teacher as the "boss" of the student's learning. Of course, the teacher *is* responsible for students' learning; I'm not arguing otherwise. However, this comment effectively shuts off learning. The student will merely follow orders. Strategic behavior, like the student learning to choose a topic that he or she can follow through with to produce an effective paper or project, is shut down.

This chapter is about choosing words and phrases to present your feedback in such a way that the student hears what you intend. It is about choosing words and phrases that show that you value the student as a person who learns. It is about choosing words and phrases to support students in seeing themselves with a scholar's identity (self-efficacy for learning) and as active and strategic in managing that learning (self-regulation). And it is about giving feedback that, when possible, helps students decide for themselves what to do next.

Clarity

Clarity is important; students need to understand the feedback information as you intend it. Students have different vocabularies and different backgrounds and experiences. The criterion for clarity is whether the writing or speech would be clear to the individual student. Figure 3.1 shows examples of good and bad choices about feedback clarity.

Figure 3.1   Feedback Clarity

Purpose:	
• To maximize the chances that students will understand feedback	
Examples of Good Feedback Clarity	**Examples of Bad Feedback Clarity**
• Using simple vocabulary and sentence structure	• Using big words and complicated sentences
• Writing or speaking on the student's developmental level	• Writing to show what *you* know, not what the *student* needs
• Checking that the student understands the feedback	• Assuming the student understands the feedback

Specificity

Deciding how specific to make your feedback is a matter of the Goldilocks principle: not too narrow, not too broad, but just right. I learned this principle the hard way. I had given back an extensive paper to a student at the end of one marking period. I had read it with "pen in hand" and had almost absent-mindedly corrected all his mechanical errors. The class had an opportunity to redo these papers for credit, and the student did—but all he did was make the editing changes I had marked for him. It annoyed me to give him credit for work that I had done, but he did make changes, and I had not written any other, more substantive things on his work. So I couldn't claim there was anything else I had asked him to do, and for about 10 minutes' worth of correction work, he "revised" a major project. I won't do that again! The feedback I provided was definitely too narrow. The moral of this sad little fable is this: go for conceptual feedback.

Of course, feedback that is too broad is just as bad. Comments like "Write more" at the top of the paper do not give the student much guidance. More of what? Another vague comment is "Try harder." What should the student try to do more of or try to do more intensely? In either of these cases, students with good intentions who want to act on your feedback may end up doing counter-productive things.

It helps to use specific vocabulary in your written or oral feedback. "This is great!" is a nice, vague comment, but a better one is "This introduction to *Moby Dick* is great! It would make me want to read the book." Now the student knows what you thought was great and also *why* you thought so. This information will help the student draw conclusions about the writing choices made in constructing that introduction and encourage the student to use them again. Figure 3.2 gives examples of some good and bad choices about feedback specificity.

Tone

Tone refers to the expressive quality of the feedback message, and it affects how the message will be "heard." The tone of a message is conveyed by word

Figure 3.2 Feedback Specificity

Purpose:
• To give guidance but not to do the work for the student
• To give suggestions that are specific enough so that the student can take concrete next steps

Examples of Good Feedback Specificity	Examples of Bad Feedback Specificity
• Using a lot of nouns and descriptive adjectives • Describing concepts or criteria • Describing learning strategies that may be useful	• Using a lot of pronouns (*this, that*) • Copyediting or correcting every error • Making vague suggestions ("Study harder")

choice and style; these are much more than just linguistic niceties. They communicate underlying assumptions about students. Tone can inspire or discourage. It's important to choose words that imply that students are agents, active learners—the captains of their own ship of learning, as it were. Figure 3.3 describes good and bad choices about feedback tone and word choice.

An important point to keep in mind is that it's not kind to always be positive when some criticism is warranted or to take a coddling tone. I once supervised

Figure 3.3 Feedback Tone and Word Choice

Purpose:
• To communicate respect for the student as a learner
• To position the student as an agent (active, not passive)
• To inspire thought, curiosity, or wondering

Examples of Good Tone and Word Choice	Examples of Bad Tone and Word Choice
• Using words and phrases that assume the student is an active learner • Asking questions • Sharing what you are wondering about	• Using words and phrases that "lecture" or "boss" • Telling the student what to do—leaving nothing up to the student's choice • Assuming that your feedback is the last word, the final expert opinion

a teacher-education student who as part of her fieldwork tutored a 4th grader in math in an inner-city public school. "He got most of them wrong, but I told him 'good job' to help his self-esteem," she said. Yikes! This isn't helpful, and it's not even truly positive. It's counterproductive, and it's not truthful. The student may end up thinking incorrect facts or concepts are correct. Even worse, the student may end up with a sense of entitlement, believing any work of whatever quality is acceptable and that he should be praised for it and not have to do better. Worse yet, he may know most of his answers were wrong and think the teacher is stupid not to have noticed. That teacher will have little respect and not get far with that student in the future. It will be a long year.

However, it is always appropriate to be positive in the sense of "lighting the way forward." This tone suggests, first off, that there *is* a way forward and that the student is capable of taking it. Tunstall and Gipps (1996) use this image of lighting the way forward to characterize descriptive feedback that makes suggestions for improvement. It makes me think of students and teachers in a cave with someone who has a flashlight. This person is the leader, at least temporarily, and he or she shines the beam around until everyone sees where to go. So light the way forward: if you tell a student something is wrong, make suggestions as to what to do about it.

When you do give students information that they can use to improve, and they see and understand that they can do it, research suggests that many—in some classes almost all—students will experience feelings of control over their learning that are so positive they'll *prefer* constructive criticism to head patting and comments like "Good job!" (Gamlem & Smith, 2013). This feeling of control over learning is true self-efficacy. It is the foundation of motivation for learning.

Word choice should be respectful of students as persons and position them as active agents of their own learning (Johnston, 2004). The words you choose as you talk with students will affect their identities. Research provides evidence that teachers talk with *good* students as if they were active, self-regulated learners, but often just tell poor students what to do. Elementary reading teachers do not interrupt good readers as often as poor readers, and the tone of their remarks to good students implies that they are agents of their own learning

(Allington, 2002). Teachers support good students as they try, rather than correcting or giving answers so the students don't have to come up with them themselves. The underlying message in teacher feedback to good readers is about making sense, whereas the underlying message in teacher feedback to poor readers is about "getting it right."

These lessons that Allington learned from research in early literacy classrooms also apply more broadly (Johnston, 2004). Most teachers would say, if asked, that all children can learn—maybe not learn the same things in the same way, but all children can learn. Not all teacher feedback, though, gets that message through to all children. Monitor your tone and word choice, practicing until it comes naturally to phrase things in a way that communicates confidence in your students as learners.

Finally, sarcasm has no place in feedback. I know an English teacher who routinely used comments he thought were "cute" on student essays. For example, he often wrote "KGO" in the margins of student essays. KGO meant "keen grasp of the obvious." He was trying to be clever, but it didn't work. His students just felt belittled. If the text of an essay was trite or was making a point that the teacher thought would insult the reader, how much better to say, "I think most of your readers will already know this." Or, "Can you add any new information here?" No matter what he intended, this teacher's "KGO" communicated "see how clever I am?" rather than "here's what you can do to make your essay better."

Where to Write Feedback

Written feedback can be delivered in several different ways:

- Comments directly on the work, usually close to the evidence;
- Annotations on rubrics or assignment cover sheets; and
- A combination of both

We are all familiar with the "notes in the margins" style of feedback on papers we had returned to us in our own school days. If the comments are descriptive of some specific detail on a paper, it helps to put them right next to what they are describing, perhaps in the margin nearby. The Comments function in word processing programs does exactly this. Overall comments about a paper may be placed at the beginning or at the end.

For feedback on work that is scored or graded, annotatable rubrics or assignment cover sheets work well. Research does suggest students will be more interested in their grade than in the feedback, which is why practice work should not be graded. However, on final projects some students will want to know the reason for their scores or grades, and offering feedback can serve to explain how the grade was determined. Annotating rubrics and using cover sheets are both useful for projects, term papers, and other lengthy written assignments. Good feedback can inject some formative moments into otherwise summative assessments. It is especially useful if revising and resubmitting the work is a possibility or if a similar assignment is coming up. Then the students can use the feedback.

You can also combine these strategies. You might, for example, make notes on an assignment cover sheet but then also comment on several details within the paper for a longer assignment.

Writing Directly on the Work

The example in Figure 3.4 is one of the released items for 8th grade from the National Assessment of Educational Progress. For the sake of this example, imagine that it is a first draft of an assignment in an 8th grade English class. The feedback begins with a positive, task-focused comment that describes the organizational structure the teacher sees. ("I like the way you organized this—by time of day.") The second comment focuses on both the task and the process; it asks the student for more details and complexity and suggests adding a bit of detail to each short paragraph. The feedback is criterion-referenced. Organizational structure and use of detail are both characteristics of good writing and part of the learning goal.

Producing a second draft by adding detail and increasing complexity in at least some of the paragraphs should be a manageable task for this student. This constructive criticism lights the way forward. If this feedback became the basis for a conference with the student (see Chapter 4), the teacher could add even

Figure 3.4 Example of Writing Feedback Directly on Work, 8th Grade Writing

Writing prompt: Imagine that you wake up one morning to discover that you have become the President of the United States. Write a story about your first day as President.

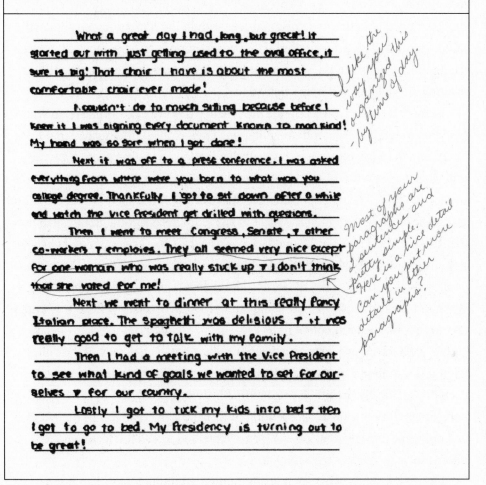

more specificity (by asking, for example, "What kinds of documents did you sign?" "What sort of goals do you think would be good for the country?"). The teacher could also add secondary comments about such things as overuse of the exclamation point as a device to create excitement.

Writing Annotations on Rubrics

A social studies teacher has assigned students to do a class presentation, in groups of four, on a topic of their choice within the period of the American Revolution. She outlines the expectations: each group will decide on a topic that is important to them, do original research in the library, and organize their findings into a class presentation. The presentation is to be somewhat interactive, getting the rest of the class involved in some way (asking questions, for example, or helping with demonstrations).

Before the assignment begins, the teacher has the class brainstorm what qualities would make a good presentation. They write all the qualities on the board and then organize them into rubrics that everyone agrees will be the criteria students will use for developing the presentations and the teacher will use for grading. The teacher transfers the rubrics onto a one-page handout and gives one to each student at the start of work on the assignment. She also notes that the Content rubric will count twice as much as the Presentation rubric for grading. Students consult these handouts when they plan their presentations so they can ask themselves questions like these: "Do we explain why George Washington is an important person to study? Do we explain why he was important to the American Revolution?"

As each group presents, the teacher makes notes on a copy of the rubric, adding the students' names at the top of the paper. She can give the paper to each group, ideally providing some time for them to go over it. She can also have other students, or the presenting group itself, make notes on the rubric and compare their feedback. Groups are expected to use the feedback to inform their next class presentation.

Figure 3.5 shows what such an annotation might look like. The figure shows the student-constructed rubric and also includes teacher feedback in the form of annotations on this handout. Notice that from the teacher's point of view, annotating rubrics instead of writing from scratch has some advantages. First, the rubric ensures that each presentation is measured against the same criteria. Second, the rubric organizes the feedback for the students. They can read the feedback alongside the criteria. Third, because of the existing text in

Figure 3.5 Student-Generated Rubric for Presentation of Research Projects, with Teacher Feedback Annotations

	Presentation • Delivery • Visuals • Sense of audience	Content • Content • Clarity • Importance
Exemplary *The class enjoyed listening! Your information about Washington's early life was very interesting.*	Eye contact is frequent. Projection and volume are appropriate. Visual aids, handouts (if used) convey content meaningfully. Class is involved in at least one meaningful interaction, questioning, or discussion.	Content makes sense. Information is clear and complete. Importance of topic (and why chosen) is explained thoroughly.
Adequate *You only asked the class to clap and tell what they liked. They weren't involved in the topic itself. Also, I wanted to hear more about what George Washington did in the Revolution.*	Eye contact is occasional. Projection and volume are mostly appropriate. Visual aids, handouts (if used) are somewhat meaningful. Class is involved, though involvement may not be substantial.	Some content makes sense. Some information is clear and complete. Importance of topic (and why chosen) is explained.
Inadequate	Eye contact is infrequent. Projection and volume are inappropriate. Visual aids, handouts (if used) are not meaningful. Class is not involved.	Content makes little sense. Information is unclear and incomplete. Importance of topic (and why chosen) is not explained.

the rubrics, the teacher does not have to rewrite the same thing over and over again ("Your content made sense; your information was clear and complete"). This frees the teacher up to spend more time on specific, meaningful feedback details tailored to each presentation.

Writing Annotations on an Assignment Cover Sheet

For paper (or partly paper) assignments or projects that will be graded with a point system, a cover sheet sometimes works well. As with the rubrics in the previous example, give students the cover sheet when you give the assignment to help them focus on the expectations for quality work. For some kinds of assignments that are repeated, you can use a standard cover sheet. This will help students generalize the qualities of good work. Book reports, research reports, and lab reports can be done this way. Figure 3.6 illustrates a lab report cover sheet that could be used for a series of labs, illustrating the annotations for one specific report.

As with the annotated rubrics, the fact that the criteria are already printed on the cover sheet frees the teacher to write specifics for each student rather than having to repeat the criteria. The feedback that students receive on one lab can inform their work on the next one. A cover sheet such as this one would make it manageable for a high school science teacher, for instance, who had more than a hundred students, to provide written feedback on labs. As shown in Figure 3.6, the teacher would be able in three sentences to provide guidance to this student.

The cover sheet helps keep the feedback criterion-referenced; the criteria are right there. A cover sheet also helps keep the focus of the feedback on the task and the process. If the teacher writes specific, descriptive comments in the proper places on the cover sheet and remembers to write about strengths as well as weaknesses, the feedback should be very helpful. The teacher might also provide some oral feedback in the form of coaching for next time. The feedback in Figure 3.6 says that analyses and display of results should match the experiment's purpose or hypothesis and that this time, a line graph over time would be appropriate. For the next lab report, a line graph over time might not be the appropriate display, but the principle of matching display of results to the experiment's purpose still holds. The teacher could check for student understanding to make sure that the student understood this principle and not just the need for a particular graph in this report.

Some research suggests that you should not limit your feedback to written text (Shute, 2008), but rather explore other feedback modalities as well. Oral

Figure 3.6 Annotated Lab Report Cover Sheet

Name _____   Date_____

Class _____

LAB REPORT EVALUATION

Criteria for Each Section	Points	Comments

<u>Introduction</u> (15 points)
    Background information on topic is clear, accurate, sufficient.
    Purpose of lab or hypothesis is stated clearly, in proper form.
	15	

<u>Method</u> (15 points)
    Materials are described clearly, accurately, completely.
    Procedure is described clearly, accurately, completely.
    Diagram of setup (if needed) is clear, accurate, complete.
	15	

<u>Results</u> (15 points)
    Data display (tables, graphs) is appropriate, clear, complete.
    Drawings (if needed) are clear, neat/readable, complete.
    Labels in tables, graphs, or drawings include proper units.
    Tables, graphs, or drawings have proper titles.
    Text describes what happened in the lab.
    Text describes how the data were analyzed and the tables, graphs, or drawings that resulted.
	10	*Include a line graph with days on the x-axis to show the changes in humidity over time. Your summary statistics were good, but the point of the lab is change over time.*

<u>Conclusions</u> (15 points)
    Results are discussed according to the hypothesis or lab purpose.
    Conclusions are logical.
    Writing is clear.
    Importance of findings (relation to more general principles in the topic area) is discussed.
    Limitations of findings and sources of error are described.
    Further experiments are suggested (if appropriate).
	15	*It sounds like you really understand what you did!*

<u>Bibliography</u> (5 points)
    References are included if needed.
    References are in proper format.
	—	

<u>Total</u> (60 or 65 points, depending on whether bibliography is needed)	*55/60* *92%*	

feedback is a common form of classroom feedback. It shares many characteristics with written feedback, especially the need for clarity, specificity, and a supportive tone and word choice, and it has some unique aspects as well. Chapter 4 explores oral feedback.

Feedback:
The Micro View—Oral Feedback

Oral feedback involves all the word choice issues that written feedback does, but it also includes some unique issues. Where and when should you give oral feedback? You need to speak to the student at a time and a place in which the student is ready and willing to hear what you have to say. Individual oral feedback ranges more broadly than any other type of feedback, from the very formal and structured (student–teacher conferences) to the very informal (a few whispered words as you pass a student's seat). Group oral feedback—for example, speaking to a whole class about a common misconception—can also be helpful. This chapter discusses both individual and group oral feedback.

Content issues are the same for oral feedback as for written feedback. The suggestions made about focus, comparison, function, valence, clarity, specificity, and tone apply to oral feedback as well as to written feedback. One difference is that when you are speaking instead of writing, you have less time to make decisions about how to say things, and once you have said them you can't take them back. If you keep in mind the feedback choices you have (focus, comparison, function, valence, clarity, specificity, and tone), giving helpful feedback will become part of your teaching repertoire. Many good teachers—and you may be one of them—already speak to children this way.

When and Where to Give Individual Feedback

Twin benefits of individual feedback are that the feedback can be specific to the student's particular learning needs and that the feedback is private. Giving feedback based on the particular qualities of a student's work means the information itself will be of maximum usefulness. Giving the feedback in private means that the student will not have to worry about what peers' reactions may be. Therefore, you help the student avoid some of the ego protection and face-saving that can get in the way of feedback.

Oral feedback is often given informally during observations of students doing their work or of work in progress. Oral feedback is also appropriate as a formal response to finished products completed by young children or for students of any age during conferences, where feedback leads to a conversation between teacher and student. For formal feedback on finished products for older students, written feedback has the advantage of being more permanent than oral feedback, so students can review and use it as needed.

Oral feedback is often a matter of opportunity—of observing students' readiness to hear it. A student on the way out the door to recess may not be thinking about the assignment you want to discuss; he may be focused on the games he wants to play or the friends he wants to talk with. Be mindful of when your own opportunities occur, too. You can't talk to one student when you're supposed to be addressing the whole class. Transition times are good—for example, when other students are cleaning up after a work session. Seatwork times are also good, if you can make sure that others are out of earshot or at least paying attention to their own work, so the constructive criticism isn't a public announcement.

Here are some of the most common ways to deliver oral feedback to an individual student:

- Quietly, at the student's desk, while the rest of the class is working
- At your desk, either informally (asking one student to come to your desk) or as part of conference time when students systematically come to your desk to discuss their work
- At a specially scheduled out-of-class time, such as after school

The following sections provide some examples of each of these feedback delivery methods.

"Quick-and-Quiet" Feedback

"Quick-and-quiet" feedback is individual, extemporaneous feedback provided to students when you notice a need. As the name suggests, these feedback episodes are quick, often addressing one point (usually about the process the student is using for the work rather than about the task), and they are quiet interchanges. There is no need to broadcast to the whole class which particular difficulty one student is having. Besides, the rest of the class is working. These feedback episodes should have no stigma attached. Short tutoring or coaching sessions like this should be routine, should happen to all students at one time or another, and should not be done in a way that communicates that there is something wrong with a student if you stop to talk.

Many kinds of lessons lend themselves to quick-and-quiet feedback. Whenever the class is doing seatwork, you can observe the students' work. Distinguish this from sitting at the front of the room and watching students' behavior to see if they seem to be on task. Observation of the work requires a close look at the papers or projects and at the students' approaches to doing them.

For example, suppose an elementary school teacher has just demonstrated subtraction with borrowing for the first time, using simple problems with two-digit minuends and one-digit subtrahends, like this one:

$$\begin{array}{r} 25 \\ - 9 \\ \hline \end{array}$$

She demonstrates this procedure using regrouping with base 10 blocks. Next, she has some students demonstrate, coaching them when they hesitate. Finally, she gives the students practice at their desks with their own blocks and problems. As they work, she walks around and observes. She looks for two things: where students make errors in the process and where they hesitate. Because it's easy to draw false conclusions from observations—the student may not have been hesitating about the work but merely taking a short rest, for example—her feedback at individual desks begins with an invitation: "Tell me about what you are doing."

From her observation of the student's work and the response to this invitation, she most likely will have enough information to provide substantive feedback about where the student is stuck in the process. For example, if she finds that borrowing is the issue, she may demonstrate with a new problem and say, "Whatever you add to the ones column, you have to borrow from the tens. See what happens when you do that."

As appropriate, quick-and-quiet feedback can also address excellent, interesting, or particularly unusual work. ("Tell me about your picture. I'm really intrigued by the look on that dog's face. What does it mean?") It still should be quick and quiet. These are individual conversations with one student. Most students will value the opportunity to have a private conversation with you about their own work.

In-Class Student Conferencing

Unlike quick-and-quiet feedback, in-class conferencing is not extemporaneous. In-class conferencing is planned, usually within a lesson that has students working so that individuals can meet with you one at a time about their own work. You and the student will have reviewed the work beforehand so you are both ready to discuss it. Because these conferences are planned, the focus can be both the work itself (the task) and the process the student used to do it. In-class conferencing could be done in any subject about paper or project assignments.

Conferences about writing can be done about one piece or several. As an example of feedback about one piece, consider this teacher–student dialogue (based on ideas in Johnston, 2004, p. 25). It illustrates what a conversation might sound like when a teacher treats a student whose writing is mediocre—the author of "Lunchtime" (Figure 2.5 in Chapter 2)—with the same respect that teachers routinely offer to students who are good writers:

Teacher: You said some very nice things about your lunchtime here. How did you decide what to put in this paragraph? [*The teacher begins on a positive note, without saying things that aren't true (she didn't, for example, say it was an excellent paragraph). Asking the student "How did you . . ." positions the student as the agent. The student made decisions that resulted in this particular work.*]

Student: I picked my favorite things about lunch. I like the food, and I like the lunch ladies. My aunt is one of the lunch ladies. [*The student responds "I" did these things. She is the subject of her own sentences, and she is made to realize that her writing is a work of her own making. Simple as it sounds, many students do not realize this about their writing; they think of it as a response to a teacher's assignment, not as their creation. And many who do realize it are not given the chance to express the realization, which confirms and strengthens their position as the agent.*]

Teacher: More details about the food for the students would be nice in this paragraph. What kinds of food do you eat at lunch? What foods do your friends eat? [*The teacher asks the student for more details about something the student has already identified as important. This isn't a "setup"—the paragraph said the student liked the food.*]

Student: I like pizza the best. The hamburgers are good, too.

Teacher: Where in your paragraph could you say that? [*Again, the teacher asks the student for a decision about her writing. She doesn't say, "Put all the information about food together."*]

If this were a brief interchange while other things were happening in class, the conversation could stop here. The most important point—that the student's decisions have resulted in a paragraph that has some nice points but could be better—has been established. If this were a writing conference, perhaps at the teacher's desk while others were working on their own writing, the conversation could go on in this vein to address other aspects of "Lunchtime":

Student: I don't know.

Teacher: How about where you already talk about food? [*The teacher makes a suggestion for improvement. The tone is one of a suggestion for the student's consideration, not an order.*]

Student: OK.

Teacher: Another place you might add some details is where you talk about noise. Since you talk about noise first, you might put some more details about the noise right there. What kinds of noises do you hear? [*The teacher makes another suggestion for improvement. It is still about details, however (and not some of the other issues in the paragraph).*]

Student: Mostly kids talking and yelling. There are so many kids, when they all talk at once it's hard to hear.

Teacher: Ah. So that sentence about the big room with lots of tables is really about the noise too. [*The teacher makes a connection.*]

Student: I guess so. I could put that with the sentence about the noise. [*The student gets the connection.*]

Teacher: That's a good idea. You might also add the bit about kids talking and yelling. [*The teacher's comment again positions the student as the agent. She had "a good idea." This isn't a setup either—the teacher suggested the connection, but the student decided to act on it. Then the teacher makes another, closely related suggestion for improvement.*]

Teacher: Would you like to revise this paragraph? [*The teacher offers the student an opportunity to use the feedback.*]

Student: Yeah, I think I could make it better. [*The student expresses a tentative feeling of agency ("I think I could") and expresses a willingness to try. If she incorporates the feedback from this conversation, the resulting paragraph will be better. Feedback on the revision should point out that this strategy (revision based on adding details) and the student's effort resulted in a better paragraph.*]

Individual writing conferences can also be done for a portfolio of work. More than one piece of writing allows you and your students to observe broader patterns in their work. You might begin a portfolio conference by using some combination of invitation statements such as these (based on ideas from Johnston, 2004):

- Let's look at your portfolio. [*This general statement invites the student into the situation. Its tone is pleasant and inviting.*]
- What would you like to talk about first? [*This comment positions the student as the one in charge of the agenda, at least at first. This conference is about* her *learning.*]
- Which one of these pieces are you most proud of? [*This comment implies that the student can judge her own work. It gives the student permission to feel proud, which cultivates an internal locus of control (the student feels proud because of her own judgment, not because you "told" the student*

which piece is good according to your external judgment). This conversation, then, has begun with an affirmation designed to strengthen self-regulation, and it leads to feedback focused on the task and the process that is criterion-referenced, descriptive, positive, clear, and specific.]

- After the response to the last question, ask why the student is proud (if the student hasn't said so) or ask for clarification or expansion as needed. In the discussion, tie the qualities of the work to the characteristics of good work identified by the learning goals. Make suggestions for further development. Then, ask the following question:

  » Do you see any patterns in this group of papers? [*Again, the comment helps the student see herself as the agent. The student is deemed capable of recognizing patterns and, by extension, doing something about them.*]

- After the response, follow up by discussing patterns that are tied to the learning goals. If the student does not recognize what you consider to be important patterns or characteristics in the body of work, you can follow up ("Here's something that I see . . .") after first dealing with the student's response.

Out-of-Class Conferencing

If a student is having difficulties that require more time than you can give to one student during class time, you may want to set aside special time for an out-of-class conference. Similarly, if a student is doing advanced or extension work that requires more time to go over than you have during class, you may set aside some special time. Out-of-class conferences can occur before or after school, during recess, and perhaps at other times, depending on your building routines.

These conferences should follow the same principles for feedback content—related to focus, comparison, function, valence, clarity, specificity, and tone—as those that apply to other kinds of feedback strategies. And they should be used sparingly, with careful judgment about how the student will receive them. I know a middle school teacher who, with good intentions, asked a student to stay after school so she could help him with some aspects of his work that she just couldn't address in her large, active class. The student, however, felt he was being punished for not doing good work. Being "kept after school" meant "detention" in his world. Depending on the school culture in your building, you may or may not be able to use out-of-class conferencing to advantage.

Sometimes you can take advantage of an opportunity and turn a situation into an out-of-class conference. When I was a young teacher, I had such an opportunity—but I didn't take advantage of it. One year I taught a 3rd grade class, and one of my students lived right across the street. His parents both went to work about half an hour before school started, and he used to come to the schoolyard and just "hang out," for want of anything better to do. If I had thought of it, I could have used one or two of those mornings for feedback conferences about some of his work.

When and Where to Give Group Feedback

Group feedback is a regular part of instruction in some kinds of classes—for example, in math classes, where often the first part of a lesson consists of going over the homework. The same feedback choices about focus, comparison, function, valence, clarity, specificity, and tone apply. Focus on task and process. Describe why a solution to a problem or an answer to a question is good. Be positive, clear, and specific. Use information from previous group work as your starting point for reteaching and review. For example, if many students made similar types of errors or need review on the same point, take some class time to do it. This can follow naturally after going over a returned test or other graded assignment. It can also be planned at other times—for example, if you notice many students in the same class struggling with the same concept during a lesson.

The following are some of the most common ways to deliver oral feedback to a group or class:

- At the start of a lesson, summarizing your observations from the previous lesson
- At the beginning of a review or reteaching lesson, to explain why you are focusing on the same learning target again and to link to prior learning and set a purpose for students

- During student performances, either live or videotaped
- When a test or assignment is returned, summarizing overall strengths and weaknesses

The following sections discuss each of these approaches.

Beginning a Lesson with Feedback from the Previous One

It is always a good idea to begin a lesson with a purpose-setting or focusing statement or activity. Many strategies exist for doing this, representing many different perspectives about lesson planning and delivery. Some are fairly mechanical (such as writing the objective on the board); others stress creativity (such as planning a separate anticipatory activity that will spark attention and interest). One of the most powerful ways to focus a lesson that is an extension of a previous lesson is to provide some group feedback about the previous lesson's accomplishments.

This approach is a good idea for several reasons. First, good feedback focuses on the task and the process and is tied directly to the learning goal. Therefore, the focus is just where you need it to be. Second, good feedback talks about the work and the processes that the students themselves used. Therefore, you are talking about them, and your attention is where it needs to be. Most students will be interested in hearing about their own work.

For example, suppose you are teaching a unit about the planets. Yesterday's work has included answering questions about the motion of the planets, including rotation on their axes and revolution around the sun. Answers to questions formed a pattern: overall, students understood revolution much better than they did rotation. They understood that orbits are ellipses, that planets closer to the sun move faster in their orbits than planets farther away, and that all the orbits move in the same general direction. However, the rotation questions were not well answered. The idea of a planet having a separate motion on its own axis at the same time as it orbits the sun was not well expressed in the work, and students were not able to solve problems that related to rotation.

You might, in this case, begin by restating for the class that their learning goal was to understand how planets move. Further, you could say that you saw a pattern in yesterday's work that suggested to you that they understood revolution better than rotation. You might ask a student or two to remind the class what "revolution" and "rotation" are, then name the specific misconception that the work revealed and explain or demonstrate the correct concept. The focus is the task (correcting a misconception). You might also give some process feedback (for example, suggesting ways to study rotation). The feedback is criterion-referenced; the criterion is being able to explain rotation and use it to solve problems. The feedback is descriptive and positive, specific and clear, and delivered in a helpful tone. You could pass back the papers, ask students to note if they were among the group that needed more work on rotation, and invite them to do that.

Using a Whole Lesson as a Review or Reteaching

If a class does not master a concept or skill as quickly as anticipated, or if a large portion of the class needs more practice, an extra lesson on the lesson's learning target or targets may be in order. Good teachers do this all the time, although they may not explain their reasoning to the class. Therefore, the students may not notice the extra session. For them, it may just be "what we're doing today," like any lesson.

I encourage you to think of these review or reteaching sessions as a kind of feedback. They may begin with using the type of feedback comments discussed in the previous section as introductory statements to focus the lesson. However, they lead to a review or a reteaching lesson. Describe the overall quality of work (descriptive feedback), and suggest strategies that may be used for improvement. Then focus the lesson on using these strategies and developing that improvement.

The difference between a review lesson conceived as feedback from previous work and a review lesson focused on the same learning target because you think the students need more work is a difference in "consciousness-raising." The difference is whether the students know that your decisions about what they are doing today are based on your observations of their work yesterday. But that is a crucial difference. It communicates to the students that you paid attention, that you are offering them additional opportunities to improve, and that the point is *their* performance, not *your* lesson-plan agenda.

If, for example, the misconceptions about planets' rotation on their axes in the previous example had been severe or had affected almost the whole group, you might decide to spend an entire lesson reteaching rotation. You would repeat the learning goal, make students aware of it, and plan a lesson using different instructional strategies than you had used before for rotation. For assessment, you could ask students to do another set of problems similar to the previous work. Just revising the same work (where they already know what was wrong and what was right) would not be as valid an assessment of whether the students truly did understand rotation. However, students could use your feedback on the first set of problems as they worked on the next set.

Giving Feedback During Student Performances

For some learning goals, especially performance-based ones, effective feedback is a matter of identifying something as it happens. For example, suppose students in a physical education class are working on basketball. They have done drills (dribbling, passing, and so on) and studied the rules. The teacher decides it is time for the students to put it all together in an actual game. She assigns teams and begins the play. Her feedback as the students are playing the game helps them to be aware of their movements and strategies. She calls out this feedback orally, as the game is in play. She may also talk with individuals after the game (saying things such as, "Work on your passing"), but a major portion of her feedback is in-the-moment coaching. The feedback in this case would be mostly about the process, about how they are playing the game. Like other good feedback, this coaching should be descriptive, clear, positive, and constructive.

The availability of video recording extends opportunities for coaching-style feedback to group presentations, speeches, skits, and other class performances. You and your students can watch a video, pausing as needed to discuss both presentation skills (eye contact, voice volume, and expression) and content. Viewing a video for feedback and comments in this way is similar to a group conference. Video recording also adds another dimension to the feedback. Many students are not aware of what they look or sound like, and seeing themselves can function as a kind of feedback. They may draw conclusions like "I didn't know I said 'um' so much" or "Look at me—I sway back and forth when I talk!" Such information can lead directly to students setting immediate, specific goals (such as "think before I speak," "stand still") that they can monitor themselves.

Giving Feedback When Returning a Test or an Assignment

Make sure you go over the last unit's test or assignment before launching into the next unit or assignment. Feedback isn't "feedback" unless it can truly feed something. Information delivered too late to be used isn't helpful. Make sure when you give feedback that there is time built in to actually use the information. Otherwise students will quickly learn to ignore feedback.

Clarify the relationship between the learning target and what you're doing when you give group feedback. Be explicit. For example, "I want you all to be able to...so we need to review...." Go over the test questions or assignment, giving special emphasis to patterns of results and the particular group strengths and weaknesses they illustrate. Invite students to review their feedback on individual assignments or to analyze their test results for more specific information on their own needs.

Whole-class feedback sessions are also great opportunities for you to teach students how to use feedback. We turn to this topic in Chapter 6, when we consider the long view of feedback. First, however, we will consider the snapshot view. Chapter 5 asks you to view feedback as an episode of learning for *both* teacher and student.

5

Feedback:
The Snapshot View—
Feedback as an Episode of Learning

We are used to thinking that feedback should help *students* learn. That, after all, is the point of giving the feedback. We are less used to thinking about what *teachers* learn from reviewing student work and deciding on what their feedback response will be. As you read in Chapter 2, feedback should describe what students did well, according to the criteria for success on the learning goal they were demonstrating, and give at least one suggestion for improvement. Suggestions should be based on the criteria for success, as well—but which one(s)? Given where the student is, what should the student attend to next?

Making these decisions requires you to understand students' thinking. The best feedback comes from a place of understanding what a student whose work exhibits *these* qualities (whatever they are) needs to learn next. It's a little like a detective story, where the work holds the clues.

To continue our metaphor of lenses, think of a camera taking a snapshot of the student work and the teacher's feedback. That picture should show an episode of learning, where the student learns something about his status or progress toward the learning goal and what comes next, and the teacher learns something about what the student is thinking. That combination will help feedback be as effective as possible.

What the Research Shows

Research on feedback tends to focus on the "micro view" of feedback—characteristics of the message itself or the strategies with which it is delivered (for example, timing). Panning out to the camera shot allows our lens to focus on the learning embodied in a feedback episode. This section describes some of the literature on formative assessment and on the regulation of learning to support the notion of feedback as an episode of learning.

The Role of Feedback in Effective Formative Assessment

Teachers who are expert at formative assessment collect evidence of the nature and *quality* of student thinking, interpret student responses in terms of what students were thinking, and consider what feedback or immediate next step in instruction will address the specific needs. Teachers who are *not* expert at formative assessment collect evidence of the *quantity* of student performance, evaluate the correctness of responses, and reteach topics based on percent correct. This is why the notion of "feedback as an episode of learning" for both teacher and student is so important.

For example, consider a teacher whose students are working on adding mixed numbers. A teacher who is an expert at formative assessment—and will be expert at giving her students feedback, which is one of the most important elements of formative assessment—will look at students' work and try to figure out what they are doing right and what they are doing wrong. Maybe some students are having trouble rendering mixed numbers as improper fractions, while others are having trouble making the fractions compatible (same denominator), and others are having trouble adding the fractions once they are compatible. These students should get different feedback. A teacher who is not expert in formative assessment will note which students got a lot of the problems wrong and put those students in a group to "work on mixed numbers." This will help a little, but won't be nearly as effective as taking each student's thinking from where it is to where it needs to be.

Minstrell, Anderson, and Li (2009) conducted professional development and videotaped science teachers using the formative assessment process. They found that although different teachers may appear to be following the same formative assessment steps—gathering data, interpreting it, and acting on the findings—underlying intentions and purposes made a big difference in the quality of their work. Less effective formative assessment was characterized by teachers' actions, even if they were doing student activities, and typically answered the question "How many of my students have 'got it'?" For students who did not "get it," teachers assigned a review. More effective formative assessment was characterized by teachers asking what students were thinking in relation to learning goals, interpreting the strengths and problem areas in their thinking, and then designing feedback or additional learning experiences for students to target those diagnosed needs.

Kroog, Ruiz-Primo, and Sands (2014) observed science and mathematics teachers' use of formative assessment. Like Minstrell and his colleagues, they were able to rate teachers' lessons from high to low on implementation and effectiveness, and then see how the videotaped lessons differed. They found that teachers who are expert in formative assessment spend the first day of a class helping students understand what learning goals are and why they are important, encouraging students to ask questions, and teaching students that they are responsible for their own learning. Teachers who are beginners at formative assessment focus their first day of class mainly on procedural issues such as grading, attendance, and tardy policies.

Prior to publishing his major work, Hattie (2009) had synthesized many reviews of feedback and famously prescribed that students should receive "dollops" of feedback. However, by the time he published his book *Visible Learning* (2009), his thinking about feedback had broadened beyond the responses teachers provide to students about their work. He wrote:

> It was only when I discovered that feedback was most powerful when it is from the *student to the teacher* [italics in original] that I started to understand it better. When teachers seek, or at least are open to, feedback from students as to what students know, what they understand, where they make errors, when they have misconceptions, when they are not engaged—then teaching and learning can be synchronized and powerful. (p.173)

In other words, feedback should be an episode of learning for both student and teacher.

Feedback events should show teachers what their students are thinking, thus informing both verbal feedback and decisions about next instructional steps—which can be considered a kind of "feedback" in the sense of it being a teacher's response to student learning. The role of teacher feedback to students in a well-functioning formative assessment cycle is to move students' thinking from the level demonstrated in the work to the next step in mastering a learning goal. The "snapshot" view of feedback reminds us that in an effective feedback episode, all parties learn.

The Role of Feedback in the Regulation of Learning

When learners self-regulate, they set goals and then systematically carry out cognitive, affective, and behavioral practices and procedures that move them closer to those goals (Zimmerman & Schunk, 2011). Many self-regulation scholars use a "phase view" of self-regulation (Pintrich & Zusho, 2002) that begins with student forethought and planning (for example, setting goals for learning) and continues through students' monitoring and controlling their learning and then reflecting on the outcome. These phases mirror the formative learning cycle of goal-setting, progress monitoring, interpreting feedback, and making adjustments (Andrade & Brookhart, in press).

The regulation of learning is broader than students' self-regulation. Allal (2011) describes assessment as a matter of coregulation: "the joint influence of student self-regulation and regulation from other sources (teachers, peers, curriculum materials, assessment instruments, etc.) on student learning" (p. 332). In other words, student learning is regulated by many classroom elements acting together, including sources outside the student, such as the nature of an assignment; feedback from teachers, peers, or other sources; and students' own self-regulation. From this perspective, feedback itself is one mechanism in the regulation of learning.

If the role of feedback is to participate in the regulation of learning, then it must be formative, not summative. Grades, while in a sense "feedback" on student work, do not lead to further learning. Instead, comments and elaborated feedback describing the student's strengths and next steps are what fosters student self-regulation of learning (Butler, Schnellert, & Perry, in press). Feedback fosters student learning when students are actively able to interpret or even co-construct criteria for good work, so that they deeply understand the criteria and can build from feedback.

Nicol and MacFarlane-Dick (2006) identified seven principles of good feedback practice that support student self-regulation of learning. For each principle, they presented research support and examples of ways to implement the principle in practice. The principles hold that effective feedback (p. 205)

- Helps clarify what good performance is (goals, criteria, expected standards);
- Facilitates the development of self-assessment (reflection) in learning;
- Delivers high-quality information to students about their learning;
- Encourages teacher and peer dialogue around learning;
- Encourages positive motivational beliefs and self-esteem;
- Provides opportunities to close the gap between current and desired performance; and
- Provides information to teachers that can be used to help shape the teaching.

A review of this list makes clear that effective feedback gives information to both teachers and students and supports both self-regulation of learning and regulation of learning from other sources (peers, teacher feedback, instruction).

What Does Feedback as an Episode of Learning Look Like?

How will you know that both you and the student have learned something from a feedback episode? First, make reflecting on what you are learning about student thinking a regular part of your teaching and assessment repertoire. You should find yourself thinking things like "She doesn't realize the effect the decisions made at the Yalta Conference had on postwar affairs; she just thinks of it as an event at the end of World War II" instead of "She got some of the Yalta questions wrong." Or, "He is putting a period at the end of every line, whether it's the end of a sentence or not; he might be confusing sentences with lines of writing" instead of "His periods are not in the right place."

Second, make checking for student understanding of feedback a routine part of your teaching and assessment. There are many ways to do this. For some students, you might ask direct questions (for example, "What is the first thing you are going to do to revise this paper?") Also, you will build into your lesson plans an opportunity for students to use the feedback they receive (see Chapter 6). Observe students as they are working, learning about what they are thinking as you do. Give oral feedback, preferably in the form of dialog with students, as you go. For large projects, for example reports, science projects, or anything that requires extended construction or writing, you might require students to write a brief description or list of how they are going to approach revisions before they start.

The following sections describe how feedback as an episode of learning looks in several different classes. It is always good to have concrete examples. As you read them, try to envision how similar teaching and learning processes would look in the subject area or grade level you teach.

A Primary Example

Five-year-old students in Ms. Jones-Nicholas' class at Rosary Boys' Roman Catholic School in Trinidad were learning that different living creatures live in different habitats, and that each creature has a habitat. Previously, they had learned that some creatures live in a garden habitat, and had named some of those animals. On the day of this lesson, students were learning that some creatures lived in an aquatic habitat, very different from the garden.

The teacher shared the learning target and helped students talk about why it would be important to know where different creatures lived. She showed pictures of an octopus and a tadpole, animals that live in water, and told students they were going to learn that some other animals lived in water, too. Students were given pictures of aquatic habitats (pond, swamp, ocean, aquarium) and of living things (butterfly, shark, goldfish, tadpole) that they would recognize from their regular environment. The students named the habitats and pasted each animal in the one where it belonged. They also had to explain why they didn't put the remaining creature, the butterfly, into an aquatic habitat: because it does not live in water.

Ms. Jones-Nicholas reported two conversations she had, one with a successful student and one with an unsuccessful student. Both illustrate how feedback events are episodes of learning for the teacher and the student. The successful student, Bobby, answered questions and spoke with his peers with confidence. The teacher inferred that Bobby knew that he understood that some animals live in water and knew that he could explain that meant water was a habitat for some animals. Bobby was able to explain the learning target for the lesson, and also to explain that the butterfly didn't fit because it lived on the land and not on the water. In addition to learning that Bobby was confident in his thinking, Ms. Jones-Nicholas learned, as she was giving feedback to Bobby about his understanding of habitats, that he liked to watch the National Geographic and Animal Planet channels on television at home.

Stuart, the unsuccessful student, placed the butterfly in the pond and referred to the pond as the zoo. He didn't understand the word *aquatic* despite the fact that the lesson had defined it as "in water." Ms. Jones-Nicholas inferred from what Stuart said and did that he lacked the background experiences the other students had. If he wasn't familiar with the animals and places, he was not ready to link them together. Ms. Jones-Nicholas reports this feedback dialog. Notice that she has chosen to scaffold some of the background knowledge and experience that the other students had, but which she has learned Stuart did not have:

Teacher: Stuart, do you have a pet?
Stuart: Yes, Miss.
Teacher: What type of pet do you have?
Stuart: A dog.
Teacher: And where does your pet live?
Stuart: In a kennel.
Teacher: OK. Good job. You're on the right track. Give me a high-five, buddy. Does the kennel have water for the dog to swim in?
Stuart: No, Miss.

Teacher: Do you know any animal that lives or swims in water?

Stuart: A fish.

Teacher: Good thinking. I like your choice. What would happen if a fish lived on land?

Stuart: It would die because it needs to be in water.

Teacher: That is an awesome response. Now I want you to pay attention to this video presentation. After this video, you will have a better understanding of what an aquatic habitat is and what is not an aquatic habitat. You will see animals that live in water and those that do not live in water as well. You will also hear the word *aquatic*, which means water.

After he viewed the video, the teacher asked Stuart to explain in his own words what he needed to do to complete his work. Ms. Jones-Nicholas' guiding questions helped him comprehend the task at hand. The point for this chapter is that the teacher based her guiding questions on what she had learned about Stuart's thinking. This information allowed her to focus her next round of feedback just where he needed it.

An Elementary Example

Fifth grade students are learning to multiply mixed numbers. In previous lessons, they have learned that mixed numbers can be converted to improper fractions, and vice versa. They have also learned that multiplying fractions is a mathematical procedure that allows you to calculate the value that results when you take a fraction of another fraction. For example, one-half of one-third is one-sixth, which can be shown by drawing a third and coloring in half of it, but also can be shown by calculating $\frac{1}{2} \times \frac{1}{3} = \frac{1}{6}$.

Today they are extending their learning by combining these two concepts. To multiply mixed numbers, convert them to fractions, then multiply as you would for any fraction: multiply the numerators and multiply the denominators. The teacher demonstrates this, then the students do some examples together on their whiteboards. Finally, the teacher gives the students a set of five problems with instructions to work individually to solve the problems and explain each step.

One student solves the problems independently, using the appropriate steps, but is not able to explain the steps. From observing her work, the teacher learns that the student understands the mathematical procedure but has trouble with mathematical communication. Therefore, the teacher asks the student what she did in her first step. The student answers, "I converted these to these," pointing first at the mixed numbers and then at the improper fractions. The teacher further hypothesizes that the mathematical vocabulary might be the stumbling block. So she asks, "What do you call this?" while pointing to the mixed number.

"Mixed number," the student replies.

"And what do you call this?" returns the teacher, pointing to the improper fraction.

The student replies, "I don't know."

After some more scaffolding questions, the student is able to explain step one as "I changed the mixed numbers to fractions."

Another student working on the same problem set is converting mixed numbers to improper fractions by multiplying the whole number and the numerator instead of the denominator. By observing him work, the teacher learns that he does not know this procedural step, and probably also does not know that the denominator in a fraction describes the number of parts in a whole.

Having learned something different about this student's thinking than the previous student's thinking, the teacher gives him very different feedback. She works through an example of the conversion process with the student, having him draw diagrams that show the fractions so he can see why the whole number and denominator are multiplied together. Then she asks him to explain to her in his own words what he has just drawn, to check for understanding.

As these two students show, teachers can learn very different things about students' thinking during feedback events. Giving feedback should be an episode of learning for both the teacher and the student. The teacher learns what the student is thinking; the student learns the next step forward in his journey toward a learning goal.

A Middle School Counterexample

Sixth grade students are studying world cultures. For today's lesson, the teacher has written on the board, "I am learning how Confucianism influenced the Chinese way of life." She explains that this is the learning target for the lesson. She asks students to read aloud from their global studies textbook. Then she asks them to cut out a picture of Confucius, color it, and copy a list of the main principles of Confucianism from the textbook on the back.

I hope you realize that this is a poorly designed lesson. Nothing the students do will teach them about how Confucianism influenced the Chinese way of life. The instructional activities are related only by topic (Confucius) to the learning target statement and will not help students get there. Furthermore, none of the activities require students to actively engage with the material or think about it.

Consider how these problems play out in what the students and teacher learn from feedback events that happen during the lesson. The teacher might be able to learn some things about students' oral reading, and the students might learn what words they mispronounced. The teacher and her students might be able to learn some things about the quality of students' coloring, or their ability to copy from the textbook accurately. None of these things help the teacher or students learn anything helpful about students' understanding of how Confucianism influenced the Chinese way of life.

The point here is that while teachers almost always learn *something* when they observe students, feedback events should be episodes of learning for both the teacher and student *about whatever it is that the students are supposed to be learning*. Only then can the feedback feed learning forward. This can't happen unless the learning target, student learning activities and performances, and criteria for success work together in a well-designed lesson. The effectiveness of feedback depends on these things, and on the use the teacher and students make of them as evidence of learning.

A Junior High School Learning Support Example

Lauren Pangrazi-Craig was teaching a lesson to her 7th and 8th grade Learning Support students at Armstrong Junior-Senior High School. She wanted her students to write an effective persuasive essay. Using kid-friendly language, she explained that they would have an opportunity to "talk a teacher into" something—but that to do that, they needed to write legitimate reasons and win the teacher over to their point of view.

Ms. Pangrazi-Craig shared the criteria for successful persuasive essays with her students in several ways, with smaller learning targets over several days. On the first day, she wanted students to understand the components of a persuasive essay. For this, she used a model. The students read a persuasive essay together and identified the components (topic, opinion on the topic, reasons, support for the reasons) of an effective persuasive essay. Ms. Pangrazi-Craig gave her students a persuasive writing rubric that looked for these elements plus mechanics and organization. At the end of the lesson, students answered questions about the components of a persuasive essay.

The second day, the students were aiming to learn that they could plan a persuasive essay with an opinion and reasons. Students used a persuasive essay graphic organizer in the form of a plan for including all the elements. They were allowed to use the Internet to find some of their supporting details, which they put in the appropriate place in their graphic organizers.

In the following lessons, students wrote rough drafts and received feedback from both the teacher and a peer, using the rubric. Students revised their work into a final copy. Ms. Pangrazi-Craig reports that using this scaffolding process, with feedback at each step, allowed her students to succeed. With all of this support, some of the students produced on- or near-grade-level work. For example, one of the students wrote a full-page essay explaining to the principal why students should be allowed to use MP3 players in study hall.

The work of one of the students provides a particularly clear example of what it means for a teacher to use a feedback episode to learn what students are *thinking*. Figure 5.1 reproduces the rough draft of one of the less successful students' essays. The essay is, at first glance, a poor one. As you can see, this student didn't write the expected three paragraphs, and there are numerous grammar and usage errors. The student found a customer quotation on the Internet ("I love my Dodge . . .") and didn't set it off or explain that it was a quote. There is no conclusion.

However, the teacher who reads the essay intending to learn what the student is *thinking* will find that the student did understand what a persuasive

Figure 5.1   Rough Draft of a Persuasive Essay by an 8th Grade Learning Support Student

> Mrs. [name] should get rid of her toyota and buy a dodge truck. Thease are my reasons. The dodge truck has a lot more Power, nicer body style, and a lot safer than a toyota. It has the Big 1500 and a Toyota has a V8. the dodge has more power nicer Body style most people Peefer the body style of a dodge than a Toyota. I love my DoDge And all the room and storage. A dodge is safer than a Toyota. Toyota had a recall on their gas peddils sticking and the air bags going off for know resons. They could both cause a crash.
>
> All thease facts are resons that dodge is a better truck than a Toyota. you would Be making a Big mistake if you pick Toyota over dodge. I Hope that I changed Mrs. [name]'s mide about dodge. I hoped I changed her mind for her own benefet.

Source: Lauren Pangrazi-Craig, Armstrong Junior-Senior High School. Used by permission.

essay is and that he can take a position and support it with reasons and details. His position is that one of his teachers should get a Dodge truck, reasoning that in power, body style, and safety, the truck compared favorably to the teacher's Toyota. For each category, the student provided supporting details: Regarding power, he named and compared the engine types, to the advantage of the Dodge. Regarding body style, he claimed that most people like the Dodge style better than the Toyota and supported it with a customer quotation. Regarding safety, he pointed out that Toyota has had two recalls.

What the teacher can learn from this is that, at least in a topic area of interest—as cars apparently are for this student—the student can take a position, articulate reasons, and support them with logic and details. The teacher learns that the student does understand persuasion. What the student still needs to learn is how to extend his good thoughts into more elaborated sentences and paragraphs, and how to improve his mechanics. The teacher's feedback to the student can be extremely positive about the art of persuasion, and she set as the student's next task organizing these thoughts into a more polished essay.

Contrast this feedback that arises from using student work to figure out what the student is thinking with the more conventional "red-pen" approach. When you read it carefully, there is actually more right about this essay than there is wrong, and the student needs to know that.

Although I won't reprint the final essay here, I can tell you that it was hugely better than the rough draft. Why? Because the student got timely feedback on appropriate criteria, the teacher learned what he was thinking, and he had a chance to use the feedback to produce a very nice essay.

A High School Example

Tenth graders are learning how to solve a system of two equations with two variables. For example:

$$x + 2y = 2x - 5$$
$$x - y = 3$$

There are several ways to solve this system of equations. Students could isolate one variable in one of the equations and substitute it into the other equation. They could put the two equations together to cancel one of the variables and solve for the other. They could graph the two equations on the same coordinate plane and find the point of intersection. Today's lesson is about graphing the two equations and finding the intersection. Students are given problems to solve, in groups, and are asked to produce a graph, an explanation of the graph and the reasoning behind the solution, and a check on their work by using one of the algebraic ways to solve the equation.

The teacher who planned this lesson had learning about student thinking on her mind from the beginning. It would be easy to teach this unit on solving equations as a series of procedures to learn, but the teacher wanted to have students think more deeply than that. She designed this activity so that students would have to show the same work in both graphical and algebraic form, and explain their reasoning. To design this activity, the teacher found a worksheet with "systems of equations to solve" and added the extra directions. Simply solving the systems of equations would not have given her the evidence she wanted in order to have a window into student thinking.

The students came up with some interesting explanations. Some pointed out that a Cartesian plane is formed by "crossing" two number lines so you can plot x and y at the same time, and likened that to solving one-variable problems using a number line. Some pointed out that each line represents the relationship between two variables as described in an equation, so logically the only solution common to both of them is the point of intersection. The teacher was able to use these windows into student thinking as part of the class discussion ("Do you agree with . . . ?" "Can you add anything to . . . ?"), which became part of the feedback.

A few students were able to solve the equations using the procedures they had been taught but not to reason with the examples. For these students, the teacher realized that their "thinking" about mathematics was procedural, and they needed more work on modeling and quantitative reasoning. A few other students were not able to solve the equations at all. Some of them made computation errors; others made procedural errors. For these students, the teacher also realized where she needed to target feedback and her next instructional moves.

The work of these students illustrates two points. First, looking analytically at student work in order to understand student thinking leads to more effective and economical feedback, in the form of both words and instructional decisions. Second, it is more effective to look at student work analytically if the assignment has been designed to let student thinking show. While it is almost always possible to infer *something* about what students are thinking by looking at their work, insights are usually deeper and richer—and, importantly, more related to intended learning outcomes—when the assignments are designed to elicit students' thoughts.

This chapter has emphasized that feedback events should be episodes of learning for both the teacher and the student. There is one final step. Based on what they have learned, teachers should be able to provide the next logical instructional step for students, and students should be able to take that step. Therefore, the final step in the feedback process is actually using the feedback to further learning. We discuss this in the next chapter.

6

Feedback: The Long View— Does Feedback Improve Learning?

Feedback can lead to learning only if the students have opportunities to use it. One of the best ways you can help students learn to use feedback is to make sure you build in opportunities for students to use it fairly soon after they receive it. The "long view" of feedback, using the metaphor of a telescope lens, helps us remember to focus on the consequences of feedback. Did the feedback improve student learning?

Feedback is effective if it "feeds forward" (Moss & Brookhart, 2009, pp. 44–59)—if it "is used by the learner in improving performance" (Wiliam, 2011, p. 120). Actually, there is still debate in the field of formative assessment as to what constitutes "formative"—does the feedback have to change performance or is it enough that the feedback *could* be used to change performance? To my mind, this distinction matters little when you are giving feedback to a student with the intention of feeding learning forward. If some positive consequence for learning does not ensue, then the feedback has failed in its purpose. That doesn't have to be cause for weeping and wailing—just keep trying. Try to learn from the failure. What was the cause? Did the student not understand the feedback? Was the feedback too much or too little? Did the student understand but not have an opportunity to do revisions or do further studying in a timely fashion? Whatever the cause, learn from it and adjust your feedback accordingly.

What the Research Shows

I'd like to start the research section of this chapter with a personal story. I have done some research about students' uses of formative assessment information myself. I was interested in how students interpret the feedback that is available to them and what they do with it. This research was part of a broader research agenda that sought to describe how classroom assessments of various sorts affected student learning and motivation. As part of that research, I interviewed elementary, middle, and high school students about their classroom assessments and their responses to them. The story I will tell here is about the high school students.

I visited classes in two high schools, and I talked with a variety of students. They ranged in socioeconomic background, attendance and behavior records, health and well-being, attitudes toward school—everything you can imagine. One of the things that struck me the most was that the successful students, most of whom were college-bound and intentionally applied themselves to their studies, used every bit of information they could get—whether it was intentional feedback or not—to move their learning forward. If students are to improve, they must develop an increasingly complex understanding of themselves as learners, of their learning goals and the criteria for success, and of strategies that help them improve. Successful students test their concepts of themselves as learners and of the quality of their work against the evidence they get in their feedback. Successful students are willing to have the quality of their work confirmed or challenged, knowing they have the means to meet the challenge (Brookhart, 2001). Conversely, the less successful students were more likely to see assessment and feedback as under their teacher's control, not their own.

I wish you could have been there with me as I talked with the successful students. If you are a teacher, you have met some of these students yourself. There was the shy senior in the Anatomy class who had just heard the day before that she was accepted into Harvard. There was the ebullient sophomore in an English class who acknowledged that he didn't think he was going to enjoy a poetry-writing assignment because he didn't really like poetry, but once he got into it found that "it wasn't that bad and I enjoyed it" (Brookhart, 2001, p. 165). There was the sweet 11th grader who used her interview and research assignment to find out more about what life must have been like for her great-grandfather, who had died two years before. These students, with the help of their teachers, all saw that the information about their learning conveyed by their classroom assessments was useful to them. They all figured out ways to use the information themselves. It was so wonderful to share the insights of these proactive, self-regulated learners.

One of the main points of this chapter is that you can scaffold this kind of experience with formative feedback for all students. You can, and should, deliberately plan lessons that include opportunities for students to use feedback. These opportunities can be structured to help students learn how to self-regulate—how to monitor their learning, incorporate feedback into their thinking, and adjust their next steps.

Some research suggests that the weakest link in the formative assessment chain is teachers' use of feedback. Heritage, Kim, Vendlinski, and Herman (2009) found that teachers were better at drawing conclusions about students' understanding from assessment information than they were at designing the next steps in instruction. If teachers have a hard time deciding on the next step based on formative assessment information, how much harder will it be for students? And yet some teachers routinely give students feedback that they intend to be used "next time" they do something.

"Next time" feedback is ineffective. The longer the time between receiving feedback and recalling it, much less using it, the more the feedback message fades from specific descriptions and suggestions to a general memory of evaluation. As much as we would like to believe it, students will not memorize our feedback and call it to mind the next time it is relevant. We have to structure those opportunities for students by planning immediate opportunities for students to use the feedback. We have to take the "long view" for feedback to be effective.

Recall from Chapter 5 that the last phase of the self-regulation of learning process is reaction and reflection. The last phase of the formative assessment cycle is "Where to next?" Taking the long view of feedback, not just giving feedback but following up with opportunities for students to use it, connects theory and practice. And, simply, it works.

Strategies for Helping Students Use Feedback

Using feedback from teachers does not come naturally to all students, but you can teach them to do it. You can also harness the usefulness of the feedback that comes from self- and peer assessment, both of which have their place and also their limits. Figure 6.1 summarizes the strategies discussed here.

Figure 6.1   Strategies to Help Students Learn to Use Feedback

- Model giving and using feedback yourself.
- Teach students where feedback comes from.
- Teach students self- and peer-assessment skills.
- Increase students' interest in feedback because they own it.
- Teach students to answer their own questions and develop self-regulation skills, necessary for using any feedback.
- Be clear about the learning target and the criteria for good work.
- Use assignments with obvious value and interest.
- Explain to students why an assignment is given.
- Make directions clear.
- Use clear rubrics.
- Have students develop their own rubrics, or translate yours into "kid-friendly" language.
- Design lessons that incorporate using the rubrics as students work.
- Design lessons in which students use feedback on previous work to produce better work.
- Provide opportunities for students to redo complex assignments.
- Give new but similar assignments for less complex learning targets.
- Give opportunities for students to make connections between the feedback they receive and the improvement in their work.

Ideally, both self-assessment (internal feedback) and teacher feedback (external feedback) should help students control their learning. New concepts and skills will require more teacher regulation, including teacher feedback that describes performance and also suggests strategies for improvement. The strategies you suggest and model will become part of the students' repertoire for practicing that skill. The criteria you describe in your feedback will become part of the students' own criteria for viewing that kind of work. Gradually more and more self-assessment should occur: as concepts become more familiar, students come up with their own learning strategies, and less teacher feedback is needed.

Modeling How to Give and Use Feedback

Modeling is one of the best ways to teach. It's more than a classroom strategy; it's embodied in our culture, in sayings we use all the time to illustrate life lessons. "Practice what you preach" charges people to model. "Do as I say, not as I do" is an admission that when we don't practice what we preach, there is little reason for others to do what we advocate.

You can model giving and using feedback as part of lessons. I once observed a high school poetry lesson during which the teacher showed students a poem she had written, the comments of a friend, and then the revisions she had made. The students discussed why the changes were improvements and what the teacher had done in order to follow the suggestions. She provided something of a think-aloud about her decisions as a writer as she revised her poem after the feedback. She described what she was trying to express (it was a poem about darkness) and what effect she wanted the poem to have on her readers. Then she described the process of considering each suggestion with that in mind and deciding how to revise her poem accordingly.

You can also model openness to criticism by creating a classroom environment in which constructive criticism is expected and where "mistakes" are recognized as opportunities to learn—for you as well as your students. You express this attitude in your tone of voice and type of comment, in the opportunities for revising work and demonstrating improvement that you provide, and in your handling of that improvement. If a student is made to feel bad even after demonstrating improvement, openness to further constructive criticism is less likely.

Teaching Self-Assessment Skills

Self- and peer-assessment skills may not come naturally. These skills are best taught in context, in lessons that use a self-assessment strategy to provide students with information about their own work that they can see is useful and helps them improve. This approach teaches students where feedback comes from. They will learn the strategy at the same time as they learn how to improve their project, writing assignment, math problem solving, or whatever they are working on.

Self-assessment increases students' interest in feedback because the feedback is "theirs"; it answers their own questions and helps them to develop the self-regulation skills necessary for using any feedback. Some research evidence suggests that self-assessment is more powerful for learning than peer assessment (Sadler & Good, 2006). The reason seems to be related to self-regulation. In self-assessment, students practice how to monitor, evaluate, and make plans about their own work in relation to a learning target. This, of course, is the goal of learning, whether it's called "self-assessment" or not.

Reviews of the self-assessment research (Andrade & Brown, 2016; Andrade & Valtcheva, 2009; Brown & Harris, 2013; Falchikov & Boud, 1989; Ross, 2006) report that students who are more competent self-assessors are more humble in their self-evaluations. High achievers tend to underestimate, while low achievers tend to overestimate, their performance as compared with teacher ratings. And in general, most students are accurate in their evaluation of how well they have done on tests. Training and practice in self-assessment, opportunities to discuss criteria, the nature of the task and criteria (simple and concrete tasks work best), and experience with the subject, as well as age and student ability, all affect the quality of self-assessment.

Andrade and Valtcheva (2009) argued that self-assessment can increase both learning and self-regulation of learning. They also found that students' attitudes toward self-assessment were only negative when the self-assessment was used for grading (summative assessment). Ross (2006) and Brown and Harris (2013) also emphasize the intimate connection between self-assessment and self-regulation of learning. Self-assessment enhances an internal locus of control, supports self-referencing over norm-referencing, and leads to improved self-efficacy, engagement, behavior, and student-teacher relationships.

An Example from Elementary Math

One way to help students organize self-assessment and use it as feedback is to have them keep records of their performance and reflect on it. In one 3rd grade class, a teacher had her students make bar graphs to record each successive week of quiz scores on the multiplication facts, for 10 weeks. They also predicted how they would do the following week. Figure 6.2 shows what these "Minute Math" graphs looked like.

In conjunction with the graphs, the teacher used a lesson plan designed to help the students reflect on their performance and make plans for what to do to improve the next week. Each week as they were doing their graphing, she asked them to think about where they were now (their current quiz score), their goal (their predicted quiz score for the next week and something they needed to *learn* to reach it (for example, "my seven tables")), and what they would do to reach their goal. To start their thinking, she gave them choices of study strategies that might help: study flash cards, play multiplication games, study with parents, write a number sentence, use repeated addition, draw a picture, or make an array. Students had to say which of these was the strategy they had used most last week; say how well they had followed through with that strategy; decide whether the strategy was working or not; and, based on that decision, plan to either stick with their strategy or switch to a new one. The following week they had the opportunity to evaluate again how well their strategy worked.

Notice that in this series of lessons the teacher didn't *give* the feedback herself. She was not in a position to know the feedback information that was needed—which study strategies each student had used and whether they had

Figure 6.2 "Minute Math" Student Graph

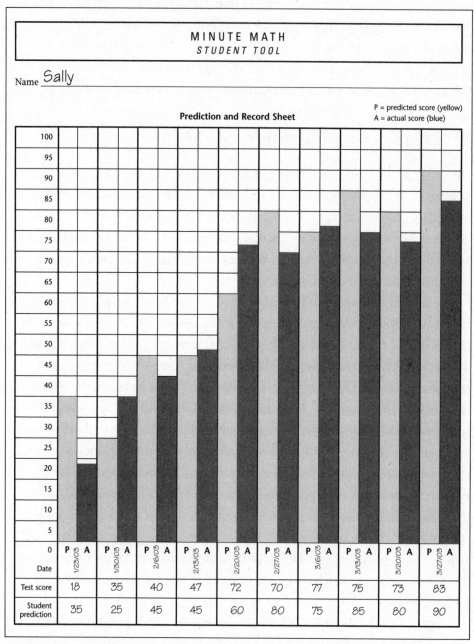

MINUTE MATH
STUDENT TOOL

Name Sally

Prediction and Record Sheet

P = predicted score (yellow)
A = actual score (blue)

Date	1/23/03	1/30/03	2/6/03	2/13/03	2/20/03	2/27/03	3/6/03	3/13/03	3/20/03	3/27/03
Test score	18	35	40	47	72	70	77	75	73	83
Student prediction	35	25	45	45	60	80	75	85	80	90

Source: From *Formative Assessment Strategies for Every Classroom* (2nd ed., p. 216), by Susan M. Brookhart, 2010, Alexandria, VA: ASCD. Copyright 2010 by ASCD.

worked to the student's satisfaction. What she did do was structure repeated opportunities for self-assessment and for *using* the feedback thus generated. After 10 weeks, the students were accustomed to asking themselves these questions. They were used to connecting the amount and type of effort they had expended with performance. And after going through them for 10 weeks, they had internalized that list of math study strategies. These are great "learning how to learn" outcomes in their own right, but you will not be surprised to hear that everyone in the class learned the multiplication facts as well.

Teaching Peer-Assessment Skills

Research on peer assessment in higher education has been reviewed thoroughly (Falchikov & Goldfinch, 2000). Much of the research has been about peer–teacher scoring agreement (Falchikov & Goldfinch, 2000; van Zundert, 2010). However, the learning, performance, and interpersonal aspects of peer assessment in higher education have also been studied (Topping, 1998; van Gennip, 2009; van Zundert, 2010). Peer-assessment skill does not "come naturally"; training in how to do peer assessment improves its outcomes (van Zundert, 2010). Students who receive better feedback derive more learning benefits from peer feedback (van Gennip, 2009). Social embarrassment and peer qualifications as evaluators are potential issues (Topping, 1998).

Panadero (2016) and Topping (2013) reviewed research on K–12 peer assessment. Panadero (2016) showed that traditional research on peer assessment has mostly been concerned with the reliability and validity of summative scores, but more recent research has treated peer assessment as a form of collaborative learning. He found that students have some concerns about peer assessment and that a friendship bias exists in peer assessment scoring. Topping (2013) found the research base for peer assessment as a support of learning to be weak; there was little evidence suggesting that it supported learning at the elementary level, although there was some evidence that it did so at the secondary level. Secondary students questioned the value of peer assessment and noted that the feedback from peer assessment may not be accurate. Affirming and suggestive peer feedback has positive effects on learning, but didactic and corrective feedback has negative effects. Both Panadero (2016) and Topping (2013) concluded that, despite the difficulties, peer assessment should be pursued as a collaborative learning strategy. They both advise more investment in collaborative and formative peer assessment and a move away from peer grading.

I also see a use for peer assessment as part of the formative learning process, as long as it is handled carefully. As students participate in peer assessment, they are practicing applying the criteria for good work. This practice builds general knowledge about the learning target more than individuals' skill at meeting it. Peer assessment also contributes to creating a classroom environment that values feedback and constructive criticism. Because peer assessment may not be the most direct path to improving students' own learning, it should be used when the purpose of a lesson is to provide external feedback to classmates about some work they will then have an opportunity to revise.

Ground Rules for Peer Editing

Peer editing of writing or peer review of projects or assignments can be fun for all and a great source of second opinions, or it can be a waste of time. Peer editing skills improve with practice, and some ground rules help. You could make a list of ground rules and post them or pass them out as a handout. The list in Figure 6.3 is just a suggestion; adjust the list for your own students.

Figure 6.3 Ground Rules for Peer Editing

- Read your peer's work carefully.
- Compare the work with the rubric.
- Talk about the work, not the person.
- Don't judge (e.g., don't say, "That's bad"); rather, describe what you think is good about the work and what's missing or could be done better.
- Make specific suggestions.
- Tell what you think, and then ask what the author thinks.

Ground rules for peer editing can become the basis for a role-play lesson. Select a pair of students (or a larger group—however many students you use to peer edit) to role-play peer editing in front of the class. Give each student a copy of your ground rules, and give each of the role-play students a copy of some work—either real work or something everyone would be familiar with, such as "Little Red Riding Hood" or "Mary Had a Little Lamb." Arrange the desks as you would for a real peer editing session, and ask the students to role-play peer editing each other's papers while the rest of the class watches.

Without letting the class know you've done so, ask each of the students to pick one of the ground rules to break during the role-play. For example, a student breaking the third rule might say things like "You idiot! This is the worst paper I ever saw!" A student breaking the fifth rule might say something like "This is nice" and not give any more feedback, such as explaining why it was nice or what to do next. After the role-play, ask the class if they can identify which rule or rules were broken and tell why. In discussion, ask students to identify the effect that breaking that rule had on the usefulness of the peer editing. Use one role-play or several, until students have had a chance to understand and internalize the ground rules.

Peer Assessment of Class Presentations

For class presentations, usually at least one of the criteria on a rubric has to do with how clear and understandable the presentation was to the audience. The class is in a good position to give feedback about that aspect of a presentation.

For peer assessment of class presentations, make sure the students are familiar with the rubric or whatever framework you are using to structure the feedback (for an example, see the rubric in Figure 3.5). Using some sort of rubric or statement of criteria is important for focusing class observations. Usually you would not simply say, "What do you think about this presentation?" You would ask students to give feedback about how well they thought the presentation met certain criteria. The best way for the class to become familiar with the criteria is to have them available as a guide as they work on their own presentations.

As each group makes its presentation, have class members who are not in the presenting group record their view of the quality of the presentation using the rubric and also write at least one observation. The ground rules used for peer editing can be adapted here. The observation should be about the work and describe what is good about the presentation (based on the criteria) as well as what's missing or could be done better. After each group has presented, give students some group work time to review the peer assessments. Ask each group to say what they think was the most helpful piece of peer feedback they received and what they are going to do differently for the next class presentation. And, of course, you need to assign another class presentation so students have an opportunity to use the feedback.

Be Clear About the Learning Targets and Criteria for Good Work

Establish clear learning targets and criteria for every lesson, then make sure the work students do to meet their targets embodies those targets and is well assessed according to the criteria; if not, redesign your assignments and criteria. High-quality assignments and rubrics or other criteria make possible good feedback. Feedback skills cannot make up for an assignment that is off the mark or work that isn't worth doing.

High-quality assignments and rubrics or criteria jumpstart good feedback. If students are mindful of the qualities of good work as they do their assignments, the feedback flows naturally from the process. Whatever the assignment is *becomes* the learning target for students, in a real sense. For example, when you ask a student, "What did you learn in school today?" the answer is not usually, "Our learning target was to properly use commas in compound sentences." It's more likely to be, "We did exercises about commas." If the assignment doesn't match your intended learning target in both content and cognitive level (recall versus higher-order thinking), your lesson will not end up teaching it. Further, you will not be able to give feedback on it. Feedback has to apply to the work students did, not the work they should have done.

Design assignments so they have certain characteristics. Each assignment should do the following:

- Require students to use the content knowledge or skills specified in the lesson's learning target or longer-term learning goal
- Require students to use the cognitive process (such as recall or higher-order thinking) specified by the learning target
- Specify the criteria for good work (which will be the criteria for both feedback and final evaluation)
- Provide students with complete and clear directions

Design your criteria so that they, too, match the learning target or goal. Your rubrics (or other statements of criteria) should do the following:

- Require student work to demonstrate the content knowledge or skills specified in the learning target or goal
- Require students to demonstrate the cognitive process (such as recall or higher-order thinking) specified by the learning target or goal
- Be clear to students

Sometimes assignments themselves are well designed, but the criteria don't match. The classic example is the written report that requires research and writing but that is judged as much or more on the cover page and the mechanics as on the substance. If the rubrics don't assess the content and skill the assignment is meant to cover, the evaluation and feedback based on the rubrics won't be relevant to the learning goal.

"Kid-Friendly" Rubrics

The rubrics you use to guide and to evaluate student work may sound like "teacher speak" to students. For example, "Few mechanical errors are present, and those do not obscure meaning," or something like it, is a common description in rubrics about the mechanics of writing. If they used their own words for that same description, students might say something like this: "Not too many mistakes. It makes sense."

The rubric in Figure 6.4 is for written reports. It was designed for social studies reports, but it is general enough that it could be used for some reports in other subjects as well. It was written by a teacher according to the principles for writing good rubrics (Arter & McTighe, 2001; Brookhart, 2013). The teacher assigned students to write a report about some aspect of the Lewis and Clark expedition. The assignment specified that they select a topic, write a thesis sentence, and then support the thesis with the written report.

Suggested topics included the effect of the Lewis and Clark expedition on a particular state; the effect of the expedition on American Indians; the role of Thomas Jefferson in the expedition; and food, clothing, or shelter during the expedition. Students could pick a suggested topic or one of their own if the teacher approved it. Learning to write and support a thesis was one of the learning targets, as was learning how to do research and, of course, learning about the Lewis and Clark expedition. For example, the paper was not to be constructed as a paper "about" Jefferson's role in the expedition, but rather as a paper that began with and explored a thesis (for example, "The Lewis and Clark expedition would not have happened if Jefferson had not believed there would be both economic and scientific benefits from it"). The teacher provided some resources in the classroom and time for research in the school library. The final product was to be a written report stating the thesis, supporting it with information, and illustrating it with visuals (tables, charts, or pictures). The rubric in Figure 6.4 was provided as part of the assignment.

The rubric was appropriate for the goals of the assignment, and most of the students were able to understand it. Encouraging "kid-friendly" rubrics does not mean that most students really don't understand teacher-written rubrics. However, these rubrics are not phrased the way students would speak, and therefore won't do much to help students keep the criteria in mind for self-regulation as they work. And, important for this book, these rubrics are not phrased in a way that relates to how students will take in teacher feedback when it's given.

To help students understand the criteria, monitor work on their reports, and understand teacher feedback, the teacher prepared an exercise for the day she gave the assignment. After she presented the assignment itself, she put the students in groups of three or four. She gave each of them a copy of her rubric

Figure 6.4 Teacher's Rubric for Written Projects

	Content	Organization	Written Language	Visuals
4	The thesis is clear. A large amount and variety of material and evidence support the thesis. All material is relevant. This material includes details. Information is accurate. Appropriate sources were consulted.	Information is clearly and explicitly related to the point(s) the material is intended to support. Information is organized in a logical manner and is presented concisely. Flow is good. Introductions, transitions, and other connecting material take the listener/reader along.	There are few errors of grammar and usage; any minor errors do not interfere with meaning. Language style and word choice are highly effective and enhance meaning. Style and word choice are appropriate to the project.	Graphics, props, constructions, or multimedia successfully fulfill the purpose of the assignment. Material is clearly connected to the points to be made. Points would not have been as clearly made without the materials. Use of materials is varied and appropriate. Use of materials is original and captures the audience's or reader's attention.
3	The thesis is clear. An adequate amount of material and evidence supports the thesis. Most material is relevant. This material includes details. Information is mostly accurate; any inaccuracies are minor and do not interfere with the points made. Appropriate sources were consulted.	Information is clearly related to the point(s) the material is intended to support, although not all connections may be explained. Information is organized in a logical manner. Flow is adequate. Introductions, transitions, and other connecting material take the listener/reader along for the most part. Any abrupt transitions do not interfere with intended meaning.	Some errors of grammar and usage are present; errors do not interfere with meaning. Language style and word choice are for the most part effective and appropriate to the project.	Graphics, props, constructions, or multimedia fulfill the purpose of the assignment. Material illustrates the points to be made. Use of materials is varied and appropriate. Use of materials is somewhat original.

(continued)

Figure 6.4 Teacher's Rubric for Written Projects (Continued)

	Content	Organization	Written Language	Visuals
2	The thesis may be somewhat unclear. Some material and evidence support the thesis. Some of the material is relevant, and some is not. Details are lacking. Information may include some inaccuracies. At least some sources are appropriate.	Some of the information is related to the point(s) the material is intended to support, but connections are not explained. Information is not entirely organized in a logical manner, although some structure is apparent. Flow is choppy. Introductions, transitions, and other connecting material may be lacking or unsuccessful.	Major errors of grammar and usage begin to interfere with meaning. Language style and word choice are simple, bland, or otherwise not very effective or not entirely appropriate.	Graphics, props, constructions, or multimedia are not entirely connected to the purpose of the assignment. Not all material illustrates the points to be made. Use of materials is appropriate but lacks originality.
1	The thesis is not clear. Much of the material may be irrelevant to the overall topic or inaccurate. Details are lacking. Appropriate sources were not consulted.	Information is not related to the point(s) the material is intended to support. Information is not organized in a logical manner. Material does not flow. Information is presented as a sequence of unrelated material.	Major errors of grammar and usage make meaning unclear. Language style and word choice are ineffective or inappropriate.	Graphics, props, constructions, or multimedia are not connected to the purpose of the assignment. Material does not illustrate the points to be made (or there are no points made). Materials are not relevant, appropriate, or original.

and a blank template. The template consisted of the same grid as the rubric, with the criteria titles and level numbers, but with the spaces for the descriptions of each level left blank.

The students "translated" the rubric into their own words, using their blank forms as worksheets and filling in one copy per group, with agreed-upon language, to turn in to the teacher. The teacher presented these as choices, and the whole class decided what they would list for each cell in the rubric. As needed, the teacher gave guidance and feedback orally during this discussion—for example, if the students seemed to have missed an aspect of one of the descriptions. The result was a kid-friendly rubric like the one in Figure 6.5, which was easier and more fun to use than the teacher's. The exercise also produced a deeper benefit.

Understanding text and putting it into one's own words is the classic comprehension activity. An important result of this exercise was that the students understood the criteria and therefore were better able to exercise self-regulation as they worked and to understand feedback as a comparison of their work with the criteria.

Figure 6.5 Kid-Friendly Rubric for Written Projects

		CONTENT		ORGANIZATION	WRITTEN LANGUAGE	VISUALS
4		I make a good point and support it well.		Logical. Organized. Flows.	Reads smooth!	Cool graphics make my point.
3		I make a good point and sort of support it.		Logical, but not all explained. Organized. Some flow.	Reads OK	Good graphics make my point.
2		Point is not so clear, and some info. is wrong or missing.		Some logic. Some organization. Choppy flow.	Hard to read!	OK graphics, not all to the point.
1		No point, bad info.		No logical relation to the point. Little organization. No flow.	can't read	Graphics not good or not related to the point.

Design Lessons Where Students Use Feedback

Design lessons in which students use feedback on previous work to produce better work. For learning targets that involve knowledge and understanding of facts or concepts, for example, use a series of assignments, and perhaps quizzes, that will enable students to see what they know and what they still need to understand. Feedback from each successive assignment should inform studying and work on the next assignment. By the time of the unit test or other assignment that counts for a grade, students will be at the top of their learning curve. They should be able to see how the work along the way helped bring them to that point. If some students don't, point it out to them.

For example, I once observed a 5th-grade teacher going over a math worksheet with problems to solve like 3002 – 284. The worksheet had 20 problems, and the student had done only 12 of them correctly. In the eight problems he got wrong, the issue was always borrowing across multiple digits. As the rest of the class was working, the teacher gave feedback in the form of working through the first of the eight incorrect problems with the student, having him articulate what she was doing at each step. Then, the teacher asked the student to work through the next incorrect problem himself, still articulating what he was doing at each step. Finally, the teacher gave the student an assignment: rework the other six incorrect problems using the same logic and strategy for borrowing. The revised assignment was not graded, although the teacher did review it and give the student more feedback: he had used his strategies well and had only one problem that was still incorrect, this time because of a copying error when he borrowed.

Now that the teacher and the student know the student has improved in borrowing across multiple digits, they will monitor the next practice work, and eventually the student will show his mastery on a test that will count in his grade. Notice that the teacher designed these instructional steps in such a way that the student got to use feedback for learning, in assignments that gave him a chance to see himself improving, and only then, finally, take a test that reported this learning.

Another example of designing lessons that build in opportunities to use feedback involves careful structuring of work on long projects. Build in formative checkpoints along the way, so that successive work is informed by feedback and the final product is the best each student can do. One or more of the following checkpoints could be included in the directions for a social studies or science project, for example:

- Having a brief conference after students have chosen a topic or, for older students, providing written feedback after they have written a paragraph supporting why their topic is relevant and researchable
- Having a brief conference or providing written feedback after students have developed a work plan or an outline
- Having a brief conference or providing written feedback on drafts of written reports, charts and materials or other components, depending on the assignment

Make sure students make the connection between the feedback they received and the improvement in their work. It may seem obvious to you that Sally's great work on her second paper is a direct result of her working on weaknesses identified in the previous paper. But Sally won't necessarily see that, and even if she does, her sense of self-regulation and control will be helped if she has a chance to identify the connection and take pride in it. Sometimes an additional bit of oral feedback about the process is all it takes: "Sally, I see that you really worked on adding details like we discussed after your last paper. I hope you're proud of yourself. Those extra details make this paper so much more interesting to read."

Formative Use of Summative Assessments

The intention of feedback is to be formative, to help students learn, and the best use of feedback happens before work is submitted for grading. However, some excellent opportunities for providing feedback come after summative events. Good students will take this feedback information, tuck it into their repertoires, and move on. All students can benefit from feedback on summative assessment if you provide another opportunity to incorporate it.

For certain kinds of assignments, offering students the opportunity to redo the assignment after feedback can work. Assignments that are about developmental learning goals (longer-term learning goals like writing or problem-solving) can be appropriate for revision. Students can incorporate suggestions from feedback into revisions and make the work better.

Be careful to structure the terms under which you will accept revised assignments for credit. You want to avoid the situation in which students will do something, then check to see if it's good enough, and then do what you tell them to do. This undermines self-regulation and works against all the good principles this book has advocated. Students who have done the best they could the first time and then genuinely see how to do better will benefit from the opportunity to redo an assignment—and they should have that opportunity if it is possible within the classroom structure. Give other students who do not need to redo the assignment equally rewarding opportunities to build on their strengths, in effect, using feedback as well, to avoid being taken advantage of.

Assignments that are about mastering content knowledge need new but similar assignments for the same learning targets. If students have gone over a test and realized which facts and concepts they didn't understand, for example, and you give them the same test again, their near-perfect score won't reflect near-perfect knowledge. It will simply reflect their memorizing the answers they got wrong the first time. However, once students have gone over a test, it is a good idea to give them an opportunity to show that they did use that feedback to improve. What is needed in this case is a new but similar assignment: a test on similar content but with different questions (more similar, but not identical, problems about borrowing across multiple digits, for example), or another assignment that requires knowing the same content.

Giving Feedback When Returning a Test or an Assignment

Make sure you go over the last unit's test or assignment before launching into the next unit or assignment. Feedback isn't "feedback" unless it can truly feed something. Information delivered too late to be used isn't helpful. Make sure when you give feedback that there is time built in to actually use the information. Otherwise students will quickly learn to ignore feedback.

Clarify the relationship between the learning target and what you're doing when you give group feedback. Be explicit. For example, "I want you all to be able to . . . so we need to review. . . ." Go over the test questions or assignment, giving special emphasis to patterns of results and the particular group strengths and weaknesses they illustrate. Invite students to review their feedback on individual assignments or to analyze their test results for more specific information on their own needs.

Students quickly learn that a test is an important evaluation that becomes part of their grade. For that reason, many students focus on the grade and stop there. Thus, tests are usually full of information that does not get used. An analysis of test results can be a gold mine of information, but only if students know that they will get a chance to use the information, that it isn't too late to profit from the feedback.

You can structure a test so it is a learning opportunity instead of a "final word" on learning. *Formative Assessment Strategies for Every Classroom* (Brookhart, 2010) includes a tool for going over tests as a small-group activity and suggests ways to use the information from that group work. Stiggins (2007) suggests ways to go over tests as an individual activity. The form in Figure 6.6 uses ideas from both sources and could be used as the basis of a self-assessment lesson after a multiple-choice test or a short-answer test with clear right and wrong answers. If the test is a multiple-choice test, put the key (A, C, D, B, and so on) in the "correct answer" column before using the form with students. The form can also be used for math tests or other constructed-response "right-answer" tests that have short answers. In that case, insert those correct answers (for example, "5 ft.," "4 sq. yds.") in the "correct answer" column.

Introduce the lesson by telling students that they are going to review their marked tests to see what they knew and did not know, according to the test, and to plan strategies for increasing their knowledge in the topic area. Ask students to brainstorm different reasons why someone might get an answer marked wrong. The students' reasons will probably include the following:

- Typographical error (student knew the answer but for some reason didn't mark it correctly)

Figure 6.6   Form for Review and Feedback on a Test

Question	Correct Answer	Did I get this wrong? If so, why?	What should I do about it?
1.			
2.			
3.			
4.			
5.			
6.			
7.			
8.			
9.			
10.			
11.			
12.			
13.			
14.			
15.			
16.			
17.			
18.			
19.			
20.			
21.			
22.			
23.			
24.			
25.			

- Careless mistake (student should have known the answer but read the question so quickly an important word was skipped, or some similar error related to work habits)
- Misconception (student thought he or she knew the answer but was mistaken in his or her understanding)
- Lack of knowledge (student truly did not know: sometimes phrased as "I had no clue")

Most students can identify when they made a marking error or a careless mistake and can distinguish that from a true error in understanding. Distinguishing a misconception from a lack of understanding is harder: after all, to recognize a misconception almost always means having already learned the proper conception. To use this form, tell students to simply distinguish between wrong answers that don't indicate a learning problem (typos and careless mistakes) and wrong answers that do.

Pass out marked tests and the review form and give students time to review their own work. Some students will need coaching to figure out what they might do. Students should be able to see that for careless errors, helpful strategies would include being more careful and checking work before turning it in. For misconceptions, helpful strategies would include different types of studying. Encourage students to look for patterns in their errors. Are all the "don't understand" items about one or two concepts or skills? Encourage students to be specific with their plans. "Study more" is too vague to be helpful. Students should be able to specify what they should study based on the kinds of questions they got wrong. Ideally they should be able to say whether they need to study a strategy (for example, how to do a particular type of math problem) or a concept (for example, the functions of the various parts of the leaf during photosynthesis), because the approaches to studying each are somewhat different. Students should be able to tell you what they are going to *do* during this studying.

Once students have reviewed their tests, decided why their wrong answers were wrong, and indicated what they might do about it, have a brief wrap-up session with the class to discuss the strategies they have come up with.

Students will be interested in what you plan to do with the test grades. It is best if you can arrange for their feedback to do them some good. If another form of the test is available, you might follow this self-assessment session and some study time with a second version of the test and then record the better of the two grades.

As part of this lesson or as part of the original unit, have available strategies students can use that are appropriate for the unit material. Point students to helpful strategies as needed. Problem-solving strategies, for example, can be useful for certain kinds of math lessons or for other subjects. Study strategies range from the very specific, such as a mnemonic device to remember a particular set of facts or concepts, to more general study strategies like note taking, outlining, and the like. These strategies are more powerful than you might think. In elementary school I learned that "ROY G. BIV" spells the colors of the rainbow, and not only can I still recite "red-orange-yellow-green-blue-indigo-violet," but I also remember "Roy" to this day. I also remember how to outline and take notes, long after some of what I outlined has passed out of my memory. Every discipline has strategies that students can use to help with learning. Knowing what these are and how to teach them is part of pedagogical content knowledge in that discipline.

Looking Forward

The principles discussed in this book about planning, giving, and helping students use feedback are based on research about how students learn. They apply to all subjects. However, different subjects emphasize different kinds of assignments. Because feedback is specific to the work done and the strategies needed to improve that work, typical feedback may look a little different from subject to subject. We turn next to content-specific examples of feedback.

Content-Specific Suggestions for Feedback

Some kinds of feedback are more useful in certain content areas than others. Although a brief chapter can't address every possible subject, this chapter discusses the kinds of feedback that often are helpful in basic content areas. It specifically addresses feedback strategies for elementary reading, elementary and secondary writing, math problem solving, social studies or science textbook comprehension, and project-type assignments in the content areas.

Elementary Reading

An elementary Title I reading teacher who participated in yearlong professional development in formative assessment wanted to be able to use formative assessment consistently in her instruction. She wanted her students to be aware of their own progress and take ownership of their reading achievement. Her students had been identified for special help in reading. Most of them were not accustomed to feeling much in the way of "ownership of learning."

The teacher wrote in her journal that she wanted to use specific feedback to make herself aware of her students' strengths and weaknesses and to make the students aware of "what they are good at and what they can do to improve their areas of weakness." She realized that to do this, she would need to record informal observations systematically. She also wanted to reflect on the observations and to involve the students in this reflection on their reading progress. Notice that her three goals—raising awareness, organizing, and reflecting— were two-sided. Each was a goal both for her and for her students. She wrote that if she were systematic about observing and reflecting on student strengths and weaknesses, and that if her students systematically were informed of and reflected on their strengths and weaknesses, she would provide better instruction: "Ultimately, I wanted students to become active participants in their quest to become independent readers by focusing on what, specifically, they are doing right and wrong."

The strategy she devised began with the reading assessments she already did as part of instruction. She listened to students read at least weekly, recording fluency as required in the reading program her school used. Then she recorded informal observation notes. As she wrote, she told the student what she was writing down and what it meant. For example, "I am writing down that you did a good job finger tracking today. I am also writing down that you had a little trouble sounding some words out, out loud. It's really important for you to sound a word out with your voice when you're not sure of it. You will get the word a lot faster that way." After she wrote the notes on her assessment sheet, she gave the student a kid-friendly note with the same contents to take home.

She found students were very interested in her sharing what she was writing down about them. To capitalize on this interest, and to take one more step toward student ownership, she devised a progress sheet (see Figure 7.1) to keep for each child. Each time she observed a student working on a goal— for example, sounding out a word—she made a tally mark in the "mastered" column. After five tallies, student and teacher would reconsider the goal and decide whether it was mastered or still needed work. Students were enthusiastic about seeing the evidence mount up regarding progress toward their goals. The teacher wrote that if she didn't seem to be noticing, students would tell her, "Look, I'm working on my goal!" to make sure she noted it. The progress chart gave students something concrete they could do to help themselves be better readers. From the student perspective, reading was no longer so much "What does the teacher want me to do today?"; rather, the progress charts

Figure 7.1 Reading Progress Sheet

Name _____

Date	Unit	Progress Made	Set a Goal	Mastered

Source: Sparrow Graper, Armstrong School District, Pennsylvania. Used by permission.

helped change the script to "What do I need to do today?" From the teacher's goal sheet, her older students, who were 3rd graders, were able to write down the goal themselves on a progress postcard that they could take home. Her younger students preferred that she share the goal information with them orally—just talking about it.

This feedback shows the three lenses in action. The most important thing about the message itself, the micro view, was that the tone of the feedback cast students as agents of their own learning, and that clearly showed in their talk and actions. The snapshot view finds the teacher and students both learning. The teacher used what she learned about students' reading to help them set goals. The students used the goals to help them improve their reading. Finally, the long view—using feedback for the improvement of learning—is built into the instructional design. Students read for fluency every week, and used their feedback immediately during the next week. The tallies on the progress sheet gave both students and teachers concrete evidence of how that was happening.

Elementary Writing

A 4th grade teacher was teaching her students how to write paragraphs. She assigned them to write a paragraph to answer the question "Do you think dogs or cats make better pets?" They were asked to have a clear topic sentence, a clear concluding sentence, and at least three supporting details. Figure 7.2 shows what Anna, one of the girls in the class, wrote.

Figure 7.3 is an example of what poor feedback on this paragraph might look like. For a feedback strategy, this teacher decided to give written feedback to individual students by returning their papers the next day. So far, so good. However, the "error correction" in Figure 7.3 is all about the mechanics of writing. This approach doesn't match the main criteria for the learning target for the assignment, which was about how to structure a paragraph to make a

Figure 7.2   4th Grade "Dogs and Cats" Paragraph

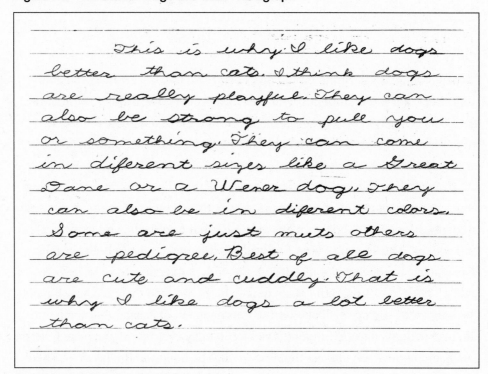

Source: Anonymous 4th grade teacher. Used by permission.

Figure 7.3 Example of Poor Feedback for 4th Grade Paragraph

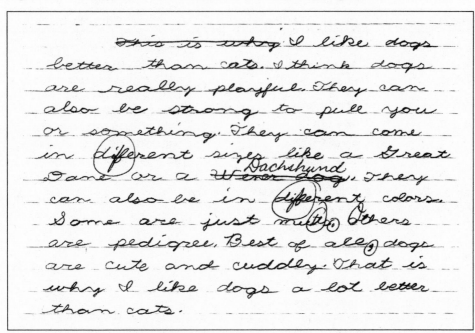

point that is contained in a topic sentence. Because the mechanical corrections are the only comments, the message seems to be that the thing to do next is to fix those errors. However, the errors are already "fixed" for Anna. All she would have to do is recopy this paragraph. Moreover, there is no guarantee she would understand why some words and punctuation marks were changed. Recopying by rote could result in a "perfect" paragraph with no learning involved.

The worst part about this feedback, though, is that it doesn't communicate to Anna that she did, in fact, demonstrate the main paragraphing skills that were the learning target. Anna successfully fashioned a topic sentence and a concluding sentence, and she does have supporting details. She needs to understand that she has done this. Once she knows that, suggestions about how to make the essay even better make sense.

Figure 7.4 shows what it might look like if the teacher decided to use written comments or brief oral conferences with the students (the latter might be better in this case, because there is more to say than the teacher might want to

Figure 7.4   Examples of Good Feedback for 4th Grade Paragraph

Feedback	Description	Comments
Your topic sentence and concluding sentence are clear and go together well.	**Focus**—About the work **Comparison**—Criterion-referenced **Function**—Descriptive **Valence**—Positive **Clear**—Yes **Specific**—Yes **Tone**—Supportive	These comments affirm and describe achievement in terms of the criteria for the assignment. They communicate to the student that the teacher noticed these specific features and tied them to the criteria for good work. One or both of these can be used in combination with the constructive criticism that follows.
You used a lot of details. I count seven different things you like about dogs.	**Focus**—About the work **Comparison**—Criterion-referenced **Function**—Descriptive **Valence**—Positive **Clear**—Yes **Specific**—Yes **Tone**—Supportive	
Your paragraph makes me wonder if you have a dog that is playful, strong, cute, and cuddly. Did you think about your own dog to write your paragraph? When you write about things you know, the writing often sounds real like this.	**Focus**—About the process and about self-regulation **Comparison**—Self-referenced **Function**—Descriptive **Valence**—Positive **Clear**—Yes **Specific**—Yes **Tone**—Implies student as agent	This feedback would be especially useful for a student who had not previously been very successful with the writing process. The feedback names for the student the strategy she has used for writing and affirms that it was a good one. Note that "the writing often sounds genuine" might be better English, but for this 4th grader, *real* was used instead of *genuine*.
Your reasons are all about dogs. Readers would already have to know what cats are like. They wouldn't know from your paragraph whether cats are playful, for instance. When you compare, make sure you think about both of the things you are comparing.	**Focus**—About the work and about the process **Comparison**—Criterion-referenced **Function**—Descriptive **Valence**—Criticism accompanied by suggestion for what to do next **Clear**—Yes **Specific**—Yes **Tone**—Supportive	This constructive feedback criticizes a specific feature of the work, explains the reason for the criticism, and suggests what to do about it.

Feedback	Description	Comments
Did you check your spelling? See if you can find two misspelled words.	**Focus**—About the process **Comparison**—Criterion-referenced **Function**—Descriptive **Valence**—Criticism accompanied by suggestion for what to do next **Clear**—Yes **Specific**—Yes **Tone**—Implies student as agent	These comments about style and mechanics (and other similar ones—for example, about choosing the word *Dachshund* or editing the run-on sentence) are not directly based on the learning target, which was about paragraphing. However, they are about important writing skills. Their value would depend on how spelling, style/usage, and word choice have figured in the longer-term learning targets in the classroom in which they are used.
Feedback about making the topic sentence a stronger "lead-in" might be best done as a demonstration. In conference, the teacher could show the student the topic sentence with and without "This is why" at the beginning and ask which sentence the student thinks reads more smoothly and why. The teacher could ask whether "This is why" adds anything that the sentence needs and perhaps point out that these words read better in the concluding sentence.	**Focus**—About the work and about the process **Comparison**—Criterion-referenced **Function**—Descriptive **Valence**—Criticism accompanied by a demonstration of how it might be done differently **Clear**—Yes **Specific**—Yes **Tone**—Supportive	

write or a 4th grader might want to read). The teacher would use a few of these but not all of them, depending on circumstances. Figure 7.4 also describes these comments in terms of the characteristics of feedback content (focus, comparison, function, valence, clarity, specificity, and tone).

Notice that the first thing to do is to compare the student's work with the criteria for the assignment, which were aligned with the learning goal for the lesson, and to acknowledge that Anna's paragraph shows she does understand what a topic sentence is, what supporting details are, and what a concluding sentence is. The rest of the feedback choices depend on the context. How much time is available for discussing this paper? Which of the other aspects of the feedback align with learning targets that have previously been emphasized in class? Which of the possible next steps would be the most beneficial for this particular student, given her previous writing? How much specific naming and noticing does this student need? If she is a successful writer who likes writing, she probably already knows that describing her own dog was a good strategy. If she has been an unsuccessful writer but has produced better work than usual because she loves her dog and the assignment asked a question about which—finally!—she had something to say, it would be worth telling her that you noticed and naming that as a good strategy for future writing.

The poor feedback in this example shows what happens when a teacher doesn't learn about student thinking, and the effective feedback shows what happens when a teacher does try to glean from the work information about how the student is thinking about the task. In this example, I don't have the long view. I don't know whether the teacher who assigned her students to write "Dogs and Cats" paragraphs gave students an opportunity to revise and improve their work based on feedback or not. I sincerely hope she did.

Secondary Writing

An 11th grade English teacher gave the following assignment to her class:

> In Act One of the play *A Raisin in the Sun*, Lorraine Hansberry portrays many conflicts among members of the Younger family. Identify the conflict that you relate to the most. Recount several incidents that portray this conflict and explain why you relate to this conflict more than to the others.

In further directions, the teacher specified the following details, summarized here from an assignment sheet she prepared as a handout:

- Title should be "*A Raisin in the Sun* by Lorraine Hansberry: Act One Essay"
- Introductory paragraph should include play title and author, identify conflict, and tell why the student relates to it
- Body paragraphs should contain details from the play and explanation, plus quotes if possible
- Concluding paragraph should restate the thesis without repeating it verbatim

Figure 7.5 shows one student's essay. It more or less accomplishes the writing task the student was asked to do, but it could be better. He followed the

Figure 7.5   Eleventh Grade Essay on *A Raisin in the Sun*

> ## "Essay on A Raisin in the Sun"
>
> I read the play <u>A Raisin in the Sun</u> by Lorraine Hansberry. I liked it a lot, but I guess the conflict I most relate to is between Walter and Beneatha. They are brother and sister, they do not get along very well, and they both speak their minds a lot.
>
> Walter has a sibling, Beneatha, and I have seven siblings. Mine are all boys, so I can't relate to having a sister but I can relate to the conflicts that exists between siblings no matter what sex they are.
>
> It's hard when you don't get along like Walter and Beneatha and you are brother and sister. If they were neighbors and they didn't get along then at least they wouldn't be living together and they wouldn't have to try to change. But Walter and Beneatha have been living together for at least 20 years, and it's hard. I didn't get along well with any of my brothers until they all moved out of our house.
>
> Walter and Beneatha are outspoken about the way they feel. Walter demeans Beneatha's dream of becoming a doctor because it's unrealistic and tells her she should become a nurse. Beneatha demeans Walter's friends. And it just escalates, back and forth. My brothers and I do that, too.
>
> The conflicts between Walter and Beneatha are because they are siblings. That's just the way it is in life, brothers and sisters do not get along. In the play, <u>A Raisin in the Sun</u>, as well as in my life, this kind of conflict just is going to happen.

directions about the essay's structure but did not title it as directed. His English usage is mostly correct, although not very imaginative. The major criticism is that he does not include much detail about the conflict between Walter and Beneatha from the play and explains it only vaguely ("they do not get along very well"). Two details that are given—Walter thinks Beneatha's dream of becoming a doctor is unrealistic, and Beneatha talks about Walter's friends—are not supported with quotes from the play.

Figure 7.6 gives examples of feedback the teacher might give and describes the comments in terms of the characteristics of feedback content (focus, comparison, function, valence, clarity, specificity, and tone). The first thing to do is

Figure 7.6   Examples of Good Feedback for Secondary Essay

Feedback	Description	Comments
Your introductory and concluding paragraphs are nice "bookends" that state your theme.	**Focus**—About the work **Comparison**—Criterion-referenced **Function**—Descriptive **Valence**—Positive **Clear**—Yes **Specific**—Yes **Tone**—Supportive	This feedback affirms and describes achievement in terms of the criteria for the assignment. It communicates to the student that the teacher noticed these specific features and tied them to the criteria for good work.
The paragraphs in the body of your essay are about siblings not getting along, which is great. But there aren't many details, either about Walter and Beneatha or about you and your seven brothers. Let's start with the play: can you think of some specific dialogue that shows Walter and Beneatha's conflict? You could look back through Act One to find exact references.	**Focus**—About the work and about the process **Comparison**—Criterion-referenced **Function**—Descriptive **Valence**—Criticism accompanied by suggestion for what to do next **Clear**—Yes **Specific**—Yes **Tone**—Implies student as agent	This constructive feedback criticizes a specific feature of the work, explains the reason for the criticism, and suggests what to do about it. These comments might be delivered together. The first one suggests two strategies (thinking and looking over the text) for finding more details to write about Walter and Beneatha. The second comment suggests one strategy (comparing personal memories with Walter and Beneatha's story) for finding more details to write about the student's own conflict. Note that the tone is helpful; the teacher asks questions rather than giving orders ("Read that play again!").
You say your brothers all moved out. Are you the youngest? Were there some times in your life as a younger child that your big brothers did or said things that sounded like Walter or Beneatha?	**Focus**—About the process **Comparison**—Self-referenced **Function**—Descriptive **Valence**—Suggestion for what to think about next **Clear**—Yes **Specific**—Yes **Tone**—Implies student as agent	
Your sentences read pretty smoothly. I think once you have added the details, one more proofreading should do it!	**Focus**—About the work and about the process **Comparison**—Criterion-referenced **Function**—Descriptive **Valence**—Positive, accompanied by suggestion for what to do next **Clear**—Yes **Specific**—Yes **Tone**—Supportive	This might be all the prompting about mechanics that this student needs. The teacher might also explicitly point out that the student did not use the specified title, and that could be fixed during proofreading.

to compare the work with the criteria for the assignment and tell the student that he met most of them. The way the teacher might choose to deliver these comments—written or oral, and at what time and place—would depend on the particular student and the classroom context.

Giving feedback to writers requires knowing what successful writers do. Successful writers state logical, interesting topic sentences or theses and then support them with details. In the examples above, this process formed the criteria against which to compare student writing and the foundation for making suggestions for improvement. Again, I don't know whether the teacher who assigned her students the essays on *A Raisin in the Sun* gave students a chance to revise based on feedback or not. I hope so. Without that step, students would have missed a big opportunity to progress as both readers and writers.

Math Problem Solving

Like successful writers, successful problem solvers use a process. There are many versions of the problem-solving process, sometimes published as lists or hints. All follow the same basic structure. First, successful problem solvers identify the problem. They figure out "What exactly is being asked here?" Second, successful problem solvers define or make a mental representation of the problem. For example, they might note that it is at root an addition problem, or a pattern-finding problem, and so on. They identify the elements of the problem (for example, Which numbers need to be added? Which are irrelevant?). Third, successful problem solvers identify one or more strategies that would work to solve the kind of problem and then choose and apply one of the strategies. Fourth, successful problem solvers evaluate the solution they arrived at to see if it is a reasonable response to the problem. The example that follows uses this problem-solving process as the basis for feedback and suggestions for math problem solving.

Figure 7.7 shows a 4th grade math problem. This is a "combinations" problem. A complete, correct solution would have nine different combinations. Further, the student would say either "No, this set of nine combinations is the only set of choices for one scoop of ice cream" or "Yes, but only if the person chose more than one scoop of ice cream." Figure 7.8 shows what an excellent

Figure 7.7   4th Grade Math Problem

Jan's Snack Shop has 3 flavors of ice cream—vanilla, chocolate, and strawberry.

The ice cream can be served in a dish, a sugar cone, or a regular cone.

There are 9 people who choose 1 dip of ice cream in a dish, or in a sugar cone, or in a regular cone, and all of their choices are different. List or show the 9 different choices.

Could another person have a choice that is different from one of these 9 choices? Why or why not?

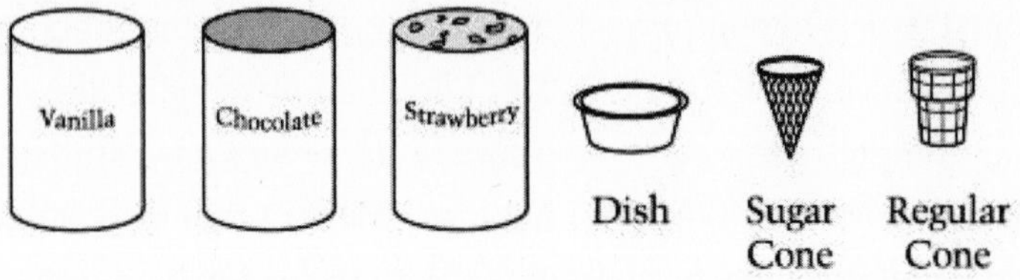

Source: National Assessment of Educational Progress, sample items. Available: http://nces.ed.gov/nationsreportcard/itmrls/

solution looks like. Figure 7.9 shows what feedback for the student who wrote the answer in Figure 7.8 might look like.

Of course, not all students will produce complete, correct work. Figure 7.10 shows a less than optimal solution. This student did not identify all possible combinations and did not answer the second part of the question.

Feedback should start by noticing what the student did, rather than what the student did not do. Using the problem-solving process as a reference, the student (1) correctly identified that the problem was asking for a list of ice cream flavors in containers; (2) correctly defined the problem as a combinations problem; (3) identified a strategy—making a systematic list—but only applied the strategy to the ice creams (the containers are not listed systematically); and (4) failed to answer the second question in the problem, thereby providing no evidence that the student got as far as evaluating the solution. Based upon that analysis, Figure 7.11 gives some suggestions for feedback for this student.

The next step—you guessed it—is that students need an immediate opportunity to use the feedback. In this case, giving students some similar combination problems, other than the ice cream one, would allow the students to use the feedback and extend their learning. The learning goal is not to solve the ice cream problem, but to be able to solve simple combination problems.

Figure 7.8   A High-Quality Solution to a 4th Grade Math Problem

Jan's Snack Shop has 3 flavors of ice cream—vanilla, chocolate, and strawberry.

The ice cream can be served in a dish, a sugar cone, or a regular cone.

There are 9 people who choose 1 dip of ice cream in a dish, or in a sugar cone, or in a regular cone, and all of their choices are different. List or show the 9 different choices.

① Vanilla and dish
② Vanilla and Sugar cone
③ Vanilla and regular cone
④ chocolate and dish
⑤ chocolate and sugar cone
⑥ chocolate and regular cone
⑦ strawberry and dish
⑧ strawberry and Sugar cone
⑨ Strawberry and regular cone

Could another person have a choice that is different from one of these 9 choices? Why or why not?

No, they couldn't. Those are all the choices possible. IF they ordered 2 scoops or if they combined them they could, but if they won a dip, those are all the possible choices.

Source: National Assessment of Educational Progress, sample items. Available: http://nces.ed.gov/nationsreportcard/itmrls/

Textbook Comprehension in Social Studies or Science

I once knew a student who attempted to help her friend with "comprehension questions" at the end of a textbook chapter. They were mostly simple recall questions. The peer tutor was a little dismayed at her friend. "She doesn't even know to find some of the words from the question in the text and then copy that

Figure 7.9 Example of Good Feedback for a High-Quality Math Solution

Feedback	Description	Comments
This is a great solution. I notice that your list of choices is in order—you did all the vanillas, all the chocolates, and all the strawberries together, and you listed the containers in the same order each time. That way you didn't miss any.	**Focus**—About the work and about the process **Comparison**—Criterion-referenced **Function**—Descriptive **Valence**—Positive **Clear**—Yes **Specific**—Yes **Tone**—Supportive	This comment affirms and describes achievement in terms of the criteria for the assignment. It notices and names for the student a strategy that will also be useful for other math problem solving. This supports student self-efficacy (the student had decided to use the strategy) and highlights a strategy that will be helpful for transfer. Note that the student didn't need the teacher to explain the strategy—it was already used. What is affirming here is that the teacher noticed the student's good work.

Figure 7.10 Math Solution That Needs Improvement

Jan's Snack Shop has 3 flavors of ice cream—vanilla, chocolate, and strawberry.

The ice cream can be served in a dish, a sugar cone, or a regular cone.

There are 9 people who choose 1 dip of ice cream in a dish, or in a sugar cone, or in a regular cone, and all of their choices are different. List or show the 9 different choices.

1 Vanilla with a dish
2 chocolate with a sugar cone
3 strawberry with a Regular cone
4 Vanilla with a sugar cone
5 Chocolate with a regular cone
6 Strawberry with a dish

Source: National Assessment of Educational Progress, sample items. Available: http://nces.ed.gov/nationsreportcard/itmrls/

Figure 7.11 Examples of Good Feedback for a Math Solution That Needs Improvement

Feedback	Description	Comments
I see you figured out that this problem asks you to make a list of combinations of ice cream flavors and containers. OR *I see you figured out that this problem asks you to make a list of ice cream flavors and containers. Do you know the name for that kind of list?*	**Focus**—About the work and about the process **Comparison**—Criterion-referenced **Function**—Descriptive **Valence**—Positive **Clear**—Yes **Specific**—Yes **Tone**—Supportive	This feedback names the strategy the student used. It is affirming that the teacher noticed, which supports self-regulation and self-efficacy. The feedback also names the kind of problem ("combinations"). The alternative suggestion gives the student the opportunity to show that he or she knows the name, and the teacher can follow up if the student doesn't know.
I notice that you list the flavors in order—vanilla, chocolate, and strawberry—twice. Keeping the list organized is a good way to make sure you don't miss any. But there are 9 combinations, and you found only 6. Can you figure out a way to organize both the flavors and the containers at the same time to get all 9?	**Focus**—About the work and about the process **Comparison**—Criterion-referenced **Function**—Descriptive **Valence**—Criticism accompanied by a demonstration of how it might be done differently **Clear**—Yes **Specific**—Yes **Tone**—Implies student as agent	This comment identifies the partial strategy the student used, and it shows that the teacher notices. The teacher then points out that extending the same strategy would yield a complete solution. In this comment, the teacher asks the student to figure out how to rotate two lists at once. There is a good chance the student can figure it out, because he or she has already shown a partial understanding. However, if the student doesn't, the teacher can demonstrate.
You didn't answer the second part of the question. How would you know if you had all possible combinations? OR *You didn't answer the second part of the question. When you list your combinations in order, you know you have all possible combinations.*	**Focus**—About the work and about the process **Comparison**—Criterion-referenced **Function**—Descriptive **Valence**—Criticism accompanied by a demonstration of how it might be done differently **Clear**—Yes **Specific**—Yes **Tone**—Supportive	This comment asks for reflection on the success of the solution. This is the problem-solving step the student did not reach at all. The first alternative, asking the student to figure it out, would be preferable if the student had successfully figured out the strategy of listing all the elements in rotation (previous comment). If not, the second alternative can be used to finish the coaching on this point.

part!" she moaned. In this particular case, she concluded that her friend wasn't very smart. It's also possible that no one ever suggested to her friend that a strategy for recall-type questions is to go back to where the topic is discussed in the text and read it over. This feedback example is in honor of this child.

To give feedback on homework or classwork that involves answering chapter questions, don't just mark answers right or wrong. And don't just supply the answer. Ask questions that suggest strategies:

- Where in this chapter can you read more about [topic]? When you find that place, what does it say?
- Do you see any order to these questions?
- What is this question asking you to do? Does it ask you to explain something that is already covered in the book? Does it ask you to make connections with other information or with real life?

After providing these suggestions, give the students opportunities to answer chapter questions again. Provide more feedback on both strategy use and answer quality. Then, remind the students of this whole process when it's time for the next chapter's questions. As the shampoo bottle says: "Lather. Rinse. Repeat."

Content-Area Project Assignments

Recall the Lewis and Clark research project described in Chapter 6. Suggested topics included the effect of the Lewis and Clark expedition on a particular state; the effect of the Lewis and Clark expedition on American Indians; the role of Jefferson in the Lewis and Clark expedition; and food, clothing, or shelter in the Lewis and Clark expedition. Students were to select a topic, locate and read information about it, formulate a thesis, and write a report. The report was to state the thesis, support it, and illustrate it with tables, charts, or pictures. Learning targets included writing and supporting a thesis, learning how to do research, and understanding the Lewis and Clark expedition.

The activity described in Chapter 6, translating teacher rubrics into kid-friendly language, should clarify the learning targets for the students and also give them a framework within which to understand your feedback. As students begin work, they will be considering potential topics and deciding which would be of most interest to them and which would have information readily available.

Because one of the main learning targets involves writing a thesis and developing the concept that a research paper is not just "looking up stuff" but interpreting the information and organizing it to support that interpretation, it would make sense to build in a first-step assignment intended not for grading but strictly for formative feedback. Ask students to write a brief paper in three paragraphs, explaining (1) the general topic area they chose and why they were interested in it, (2) what preliminary research they did and what their tentative thesis or interpretation is, and (3) how they plan to continue the work on their project. After you read these papers, you might have a brief conference with each student, providing feedback about their topic, thesis, and research.

In your feedback about the students' project plans, use the principles this book has presented. Give students feedback about their process; notice strengths and make suggestions to improve weaknesses. Keep in focus the criteria for the end product, as described in the rubrics. Make your feedback descriptive and specific.

As a second interim step, you might organize peer feedback as a class activity when the projects are at the draft stage. This seems like a logical extension of the "kid-friendly rubrics" activity used at the start of the project. This time, instead of translating the rubrics, the groups are applying them to real examples of students' work. Where they see strengths, good information is illustrated both for the author and for the peer reviewer. Where they see gaps, they can point them out ("Your chart looks nice, but it doesn't match what you are saying about wilderness food").

If a project assignment involves group work, be sure to use the opportunity to give students feedback about their collaboration and communication skills, project management, and decision making. In fact, during any kind of group work, be on the lookout for opportunities to provide feedback, usually oral, about work habits, collaboration, and other important skills that will enable students to continue to learn and to produce quality work throughout their school careers and into their adult lives. Such feedback would focus on the process and should follow all the suggestions about content (comparison, valence, clarity, specificity, tone) that apply to other feedback.

You can see that the interim steps, building in opportunities for formative feedback that the student can use along the way, incorporate the snapshot and long view right into the feedback process. At each interim step, the teacher has the opportunity to learn where a student's thinking is at the present time and feed it forward at least a little, toward the next step. At the final step, when projects are turned in for grading, you would not provide feedback except in the occasional instances where you want to explain something to students. There will be no further opportunity to revise or to learn about Lewis and Clark. Giving feedback at this stage would be a waste of your time.

Consistency Across the Subject Areas

The point of this chapter has been to show how you can apply the feedback principles identified as important for learning to students' work on different kinds of assignments in various subject areas. Whatever the subject, you should attend to the three views of feedback:

- **The micro view.** Focus your feedback on the task or process used. The feedback should be primarily criterion-referenced, descriptive, positive, clear, specific, and phrased in a way that affirms students as the agents of their own learning.
- **The snapshot view.** Make sure both you and the students learn something from the feedback episode.
- **The long view.** Provide opportunities for the students to use the feedback and improve learning.

The next chapter shows how you can adjust the same feedback principles to be appropriate for different types of learners.

8

Adjusting Feedback for Different Learners

Using the three lenses helps us appreciate the range of adjustments you can make to your feedback. You can adjust the content and message (the micro view), what you look to learn from it and have students learn from it (the snapshot view), and the opportunities you give to students to advance learning (the long view). Shute (2008) reviewed several studies of the relationship of feedback to learner characteristics. Based on these studies, she recommends that feedback to high-achieving students be a bit delayed and challenging, although sometimes all they may need is verification they are on the right track. She recommends that feedback to low-achieving students be more immediate and directive, scaffolded (broken into smaller steps), specific, and elaborated. Students have to hear and understand feedback before they can use it for improvement. The chapter provides suggestions for adjusting feedback for different types of learners, including successful students, struggling students, English language learners, and reluctant students who perceive themselves as "failures" (whether labeled as having special needs or not).

It is worth mentioning that, although this book is not about differentiated instruction per se, feedback is not the only thing that should be adjusted based on formative assessment. Instruction must be differentiated as well. In fact, I have never worked with teachers in the area of formative assessment without seeing them make this connection immediately. Information about differences in student needs almost creates a mandate to differentiate instruction. How could you know that "what comes next" differs in systematic ways for different students and ignore it in instruction?

Successful Students

Some students who are interested and engaged in learning will hear almost any feedback message eagerly. They are able to benefit from specific feedback about the particular knowledge and skills they demonstrated in a test or an assignment and also generalize the feedback—for example, drawing conclusions about how to study for tests or how to write a certain type of report (Brookhart, 2001). They are aware that they do this. Successful students do self-assessment spontaneously, whether you build in opportunities that force them to do it or not. In terms of our lens analogy, they take their own long view of learning. Successful students don't make neat distinctions between "formative" and "summative" assessment. They mine any assessment results for information that may benefit them. They are empowered and motivated by the control they perceive they have over their own learning and growth.

Successful students even consider assignments themselves, whether to study for a test or to prepare a project, as a kind of direction for learning. They treat assignments to study or to do research as formative in the same way feedback is. For example, one of the students I interviewed said the following when asked what her 12th grade anatomy teacher expected his students to do for the Skeleton Lab practical assessment:

> He expects us of course to pay attention in class; he expects us to study on our own. I guess it's good he gives us quizzes because that forces you to study specifics. And he also expects us to come in and work with the bones, and he gave us class time as well, because you can't learn 3D bones all from a chart. . . . I think it's a really important thing to get that feeling of mastering something for once. In terms of study skills it's also good preparation for college, where there tend to be big finals and midterms. (Brookhart, 2001, p. 162)

It would be easy for a teacher to skimp on feedback for students like this and instead concentrate feedback efforts on struggling students who "need it" more. It is tempting to assume these successful students will find their own feedback—if you don't give it to them, they'll figure it out. Don't fall into that trap. Successful students deserve your constructive feedback, and they will benefit from it.

In feedback to successful students, focus on the task and the process, and be criterion-referenced, positive, clear, and specific—use all the characteristics of good feedback I have mentioned before. Identify what is good and why it's good. Make a suggestion for a next step, mindful that the next step may be an enrichment of the basic classroom learning goals. Engage in conversation with students, who may be able to share interesting thoughts on the process of doing their work; successful students are usually self-aware about their processes. Especially, make these conversations opportunities for you (the teacher) to learn how the successful student is thinking. This snapshot view may be very rich.

I once spoke to a group of college freshman honors students about assessment. One of the young men asked me this question: "Suppose you were an elementary school teacher and had assigned a simple project about the planets. One of your students did, instead, a big, involved report on rocket ships. How would you grade it?" Of course, the first thing I wondered was whether this question was autobiographical. Was this young man talking about something he really had done?

For our purposes here, suppose he had asked not "How would you grade it?" but rather "What feedback would you give?" In fact, in this case you would probably give feedback and not a grade, anyway. The assigned task in this case was a project about the planets—drawing them and listing facts about them, as the young man went on to explain. The task the student did was a written report, with pictures and diagrams, about rocket ships. These don't match, in task or process. The teacher's first piece of feedback might best be a question: "Why did you do a report on rocket ships?" Further feedback would depend on the reply. If the student did a report on rocket ships because he already had done a diagram of the planets or thought he already knew the requested information about planets, you might ask to see evidence of that. If he was really seriously interested in rocket ships and just wanted to do a different project, you might provide more feedback on the report and ask him to complete the planets assignment also. If he was bored in class, you might give him feedback about his report and think about adjusting assignments for him in the future. In any case, he still needs to show you he has achieved the learning goals about planets.

But back to his report on rocket ships. After all that work, the student will surely want to know what you think about the paper on its own terms. He brought it to you for comment; you should comment, even if the report doesn't "count" to show he knows his planets. Your additional feedback comments should compare this report to conventional criteria for reports (be criterion-referenced) and describe the work. Avoid the trap of evaluating and focusing on the person, even though the evaluation would be positive ("That's a great report, John. You're really smart"). Instead, describe the report's good qualities. Be clear and specific ("The diagram of the rocket ship really helps me understand your description of how it works"). Make suggestions for what he might do next. Of course, in this case these would be suggestions for future learning, not requirements that he had to fulfill. For example, "This section on rocket fuel is interesting. Would you be interested in finding out more about what happens chemically when the fuel burns?"

And finally, consider tone. You can be positive, supportive, and appreciative of the student's interest in rocket ships without letting the student get away with skipping work about planets just because he doesn't want to do it. If feedback focuses on the work itself and the process the student used to do that work, you can have a lot to talk about even if the work is excellent. No matter how successful a student is, there is always more that can be learned.

Struggling Students

Students who don't have solid prior learning experiences or don't have the learning skills to process the information, or both, may not completely understand what your assignment asks them to do or your feedback on their work.

This group includes both learning disabled students and students who, though not identified with a learning deficiency, did not get the foundation they needed as learners (Lazarus & Brookhart, 2016).

Struggling students will benefit from feedback that helps them connect the process they used with the results they obtained. This is the sort of "cognitive feedback" that the research suggests successful students do internally. You can scaffold this process for struggling students. For example, some early literacy teachers I know point out to students how much better their reading sounds after they use one of the strategies they taught. And they teach lots of strategies: repeat reading, decoding, word recognition, finger tracking, and many more. Simple as it sounds, some of those struggling readers don't connect what their teacher asks them to do with the words and the end result in their reading. Once the teacher helps them make the connection, they see the point to the strategies and can begin to use them intentionally.

The recommendation in this book has been to give criterion-referenced feedback. The research literature shows that students who compare their work with the qualities of good work embodied in the learning targets are enabled to continue to move toward those targets. But what about the students whose work falls short on every point? It is true that they need to know their work doesn't meet the target, but most struggling students already know that. Feedback that communicates "off by a mile" or a list of necessary improvements that is longer than the original assignment simply generates hopelessness. For these students, self-referenced feedback can bridge the gap. Until they get close enough to be "on track" for the learning target to be within reach, help struggling students see what they *are* doing, not what they *didn't* do.

Self-referenced feedback doesn't mean that there will be no need for improvement or that you should encourage just anything. It means that the criteria for "improvement" lie within the student's own repertoire of strategies and achievement. It puts a target within reach. Here's how it works. Self-referenced feedback compares a student's work today with his or her own previous past performance or with your expectations for the student based on that past performance. So, for instance, if today's paragraph has two sentences—even if it's not a good paragraph—and yesterday's had only one, mention that. That is task-focused feedback; it's specific, and it's important to readiness for paragraph writing even if it isn't about the qualities of a good topic sentence, which is where the rest of the class is focusing their efforts. Then make one suggestion for improvement. Perhaps it's that those two sentences ought to "go together." Or perhaps they already do go together, and the goal is to add a third sentence or to work on the rudiments of a topic sentence.

The previous example illustrated using self-referenced feedback when you can point out that the struggling student improved on past performance. Self-referenced feedback is also useful when the current work is not as good as the previous work. For example, if today's "paragraph" is just random words, but yesterday's was a sentence, point out that you know the student can write a sentence because he or she did it yesterday. Show the student that sentence, talk about it, and then ask him or her to redo today's assignment to be at least as good as yesterday's. You may not get a paragraph, but you probably will get at least a sentence.

Suggest small steps for improvement. The struggling student may need to work on many things in order to actually meet the learning goal, but improvement is supported by breaking complex tasks into small, manageable steps. If all this sounds agonizingly slow, remember that gradual, if small, improvements are better for the student than being overwhelmed and making no improvement—or worse, giving up. Some struggling students who improve gradually will finally "get it": they will learn how to learn and not have to struggle so much. Some won't, of course, but at least they will be able to take pride in knowing that they made small improvements and that you noticed.

And when you give feedback to struggling students, be sure to check for understanding. For example, ask the student to tell you what he or she thinks is the most important point you made in your feedback. Or ask the student to tell you what he or she thinks is the next step based on your feedback. If it appears the student did not understand the feedback, try explaining your points in a different way. Don't just repeat the words the student didn't "get" the first time. Figure 8.1 summarizes these suggestions for giving feedback to struggling students.

Finally, struggling students need scaffolded, step-by-step opportunities to use feedback. These opportunities should be structured into small steps so that

Figure 8.1 Feedback Strategies for Struggling Students

Strategy	Explanation	Example
Focus feedback on the process.	Successful students figure out how to connect outcome feedback (their performance results) with cognitive feedback (which strategies led to those results). Scaffold this connection for struggling students, explicitly pointing out how their particular efforts resulted in a particular performance. This scaffolding will help all students, even those for whom it doesn't come easily, "learn how to learn."	I saw you go back and reread that sentence. After you changed it, it reads better, doesn't it?
Use **self-referenced** feedback.	If a direct comparison with the criteria for good work would result in a resounding failure, look for signs of improvement from the student's previous work. If students can see that they did make some progress, they will be more likely to persist. If they see they are hopeless failures, they may give up. (This principle is for formative feedback, not grading, which should be criterion-referenced.)	Your last paragraph was only two sentences. Here you have four, and they all follow nicely from one to the next.
Select **one or two important points** for feedback, and suggest **small steps** for improvement.	The principle of breaking up complex tasks into small, manageable steps is a long-standing one in instruction. "How do you eat an elephant? One bite at a time!"	Next time you write a paragraph, try to make the first sentence an introduction to the rest of the sentences.
Use **simple vocabulary**. Define or **explain** words related to achievement or learning targets, or at least check for understanding.	Vocabulary is a particular issue for many struggling students. We tend to think of this as an issue for English language learners. However, many struggling students have limited vocabulary. Don't avoid learning-related terms (e.g., *slope*), but do avoid complex vocabulary words if simpler word choices are available.	Next time you write a paragraph, try to make the first sentence a summary of all the sentences. That's called a topic sentence.
Check for understanding of feedback.	If a student doesn't understand the message, it cannot help with learning.	Can you tell me one thing you're going to work on in your next paragraph?

(*continued*)

Figure 8.1 Feedback Strategies for Struggling Students (*Continued*)

Strategy	Explanation	Example
Learn what the student is thinking.	When work is sloppy, ungrammatical, or only partly finished, it is easy to fall into the trap of observing and correcting surface features. Don't fall into that trap. Analyze student work for evidence of the students' thinking. This will give you more insight into how to help the student move forward.	It sounds like you really love to play four-square. Is that why you chose to write about it?
Give students an immediate opportunity to use the feedback.	Struggling students, especially, need structured and immediate opportunities to take their next steps, in class while you are there to help.	Try revising just this first sentence. When you're done, show it to me and we'll talk about how it can be your topic sentence.

students can experience success and then move on. Here is one more example. Except for the names, it is a true story.

Jason was a student in Ms. Porter's ninth grade general science class. He would say, "I can't do this. I don't understand." He would sometimes say this before he even knew what an assignment was. In his mind, he was already a failure, destined to always do poorly in school.

An assignment to write a scientific report on a lab experiment he had conducted in class was no exception. His work was abysmal. Ms. Porter decided to take a different approach with her feedback this time. She decided the main issue was that there was just too much information for Jason to deal with all at once. So she gave him his first draft feedback: "Let's write the introduction first. Answer these two questions. . . ."

Ms. Porter told Jason that once he had written the introduction he should call her over and she would give him feedback on what he had just done, plus a next step. And as she wrote in a reflection, "That was the last I heard of him for the rest of the days we were writing. He just needed a push in the right direction to help him see that he really did know what he was doing."

Jason, like many struggling students, needed feedback in smaller bites—in this case, Ms. Porter's two questions about the introduction were the first bit.

But he still needed to know what he had done well, what he should work on next, and suggestions for how to do that (characteristics of effective feedback, the micro view). Mrs. Porter and he both needed to learn something from his work (the snapshot view). And he needed immediate opportunities to use the feedback (the long view). He just needed them in smaller, more scaffolded bites.

English Language Learners

English language learners (ELLs) can be struggling students. The key feedback issue for English language learners is their ability to hear and understand the feedback (Hill & Flynn, 2006; Mo, 2007). Feedback is usually delivered in academic English, as opposed to conversational English. For example, the concept of "descriptive details" is an academic one. The idea that there are steps to problem solving, which begin with defining the problem and move on to identifying the variables and potential solution strategies, is an academic one.

Key feedback issues for *teachers* of English language learners have to do with the assumptions teachers make even before feedback is given. For example, a student whose first language is not English may write a sentence with unusual word order. The words may be in the order that would be conventional in the student's native language. Noticing that fact (if you are able) and pointing it out to the student would affirm that you understood why the sentence made sense and afford a starting point for talking. You might decide that this sentence is a good vehicle for showing the student some English sentence structure and use it for demonstration. Or, given the context of the student's sentence, you might decide that the main point of the sentence was its content. For example, if the sentence was a response to a question about a story the student read, it might be more productive in the long run to focus on the substance rather than the word order. Did the student identify the main character, or comprehend a main idea, or respond thoughtfully to whatever the question was?

It is important to match your feedback to the student's proficiency level as much as possible. Feedback is only useful if the student understands it. Mo (2007) suggests five areas for classroom teachers' observations that will help them gauge English language learners' communication proficiency:

1. How well the student understands classroom discussions (Does the student understand classroom talk at all? Can he or she understand if speech is slow and includes repetition?)
2. How well the student speaks (Does the student hesitate or search for words? Does the student ever initiate a conversation?)
3. How well does the student use academic English, especially academic vocabulary?
4. How easy is it to understand what the student says?
5. How well does the student use conventional grammar and sentence patterns? (p. 41)

Second-language development occurs in stages, from silent and receptive, when the student can understand some words but is not comfortable speaking, through early language production and the emergence of speech, to intermediate and advanced proficiency (Hill & Flynn, 2006; Reed & Railsback, 2003). Understanding where a particular student's development lies along this continuum will help you give appropriate feedback.

It is also important to coordinate your feedback with the instructional program or model you are using to serve the English language learners. Programs vary considerably in ways that affect how feedback is given, including the amount of native language use, the purpose of native language use (for a transition to English or for further development in the native language as well as in English), the amount of time allowed for the program, and the approach used to teach English.

Figure 8.2 summarizes suggestions about how to give good feedback to English language learners. The suggestions are based on information provided in readily available resources for mainstream teachers (Dalton, 1998; Hill & Flynn, 2006; Mo, 2007; Reed & Railsback, 2003) and are organized in terms of the feedback strategy and content choices from the literature review in Chapter 2. The primary point is that feedback for ELL students should be conversational. This approach assists the student's language development and allows you to check for understanding. Many of these suggestions would also be helpful for other struggling students.

Figure 8.2 Feedback Choices for English Language Learners

Feedback Strategies	
Timing and Amount	• Talk frequently with the student about the work. • Allow plenty of time for interaction and student talk.
Mode	• Oral—Have a conversation with the student about the work. • Visual—Use nonverbals (pictures, diagrams, gestures) when possible. • Modeling of English—Provide feedback on a student's English usage or pronunciation errors by modeling correct English (not by "correcting" the student), and do this in feedback for all content areas.
Audience	• Give feedback to the individual student (as opposed to public feedback). • Respect student's preferences for speaking style (which may not match yours), considering such things as amount of wait time or eye contact or expectations for turn taking. For example, some students may perceive questioning as "grilling" or criticism. Have a conversation; listen as well as talk.
Feedback Content	
Focus	• Focus on "joint productive activity" (Dalton, 1998)—work done collaboratively with other students that leads to a product, so there is some concrete work to discuss. • Focus on the product and the activity that produced it.
Comparison	• Make comparisons criterion-referenced (compare student work to standards). • Make comparisons self-referenced as appropriate (point out improvement).
Function and Valence	Be descriptive.
Clarity	• Use student's first language as well as English for feedback, if possible. • Repeat. • Speak slowly. • Use simple vocabulary; explain important terms. • Use routines.
Specificity	• Connect feedback to knowledge and skills the student already has. • Connect feedback to real life (home, community) contexts. • Ask students to explain their reasoning.
Tone	• Be responsive and supportive. • Listen to students.

(continued)

Figure 8.2 Feedback Choices for English Language Learners (*Continued*)

	Learning from a Feedback Episode
Student Learning	• Ask students to paraphrase feedback. • Ask students to prioritize feedback—what was most important?
Teacher Learning	Distinguish what the student understands from what the student is able to express—for example, try to disentangle language issues from understanding of concepts.

	Using Feedback
Opportunity to Continue Learning	Respond to feedback episodes immediately with lesson adjustments related to feedback conversations you had with the student.

As with any of the suggestions, the context matters, and no one suggestion for feedback will be right for every occasion. Several contextual factors have already been mentioned. The context of the ELL program model is important. The student's developmental level in second language acquisition is important. The student's particular language and cultural background make a difference.

The subject matter makes a difference too. Some concepts and skills lend themselves more easily to visual representation than others. Figure 8.3 is an example of a student's answer to the combinations problem described in Chapter 7 that doesn't use any words at all and yet shows understanding.

Recall that this problem had a second part, which this student did not answer: "Could another person have a choice that is different from one of these nine choices? Why or why not?" Using the student's picture, feedback could first affirm the nice solution given and then focus on how to answer the second question, at least partially, with a yes or no. The systematic nature of the picture (all the vanillas, then all the strawberries, then all the chocolates) suggests that the student may understand that the solution is complete and just needs to be helped to understand the second question and express the answer. As with all feedback, the student should have an opportunity to use it right away.

Figure 8.3   Nonverbal Solution to 4th Grade Math Problem

Jan's Snack Shop has 3 flavors of ice cream—vanilla, chocolate, and strawberry.

The ice cream can be served in a dish, a sugar cone, or a regular cone.

There are 9 people who choose 1 dip of ice cream in a dish, or in a sugar cone, or in a regular cone, and all of their choices are different. List or show the 9 different choices.

Source: National Assessment of Educational Progress, sample items. Available: http://nces.ed.gov/nationsreportcard/itmrls/

Reluctant Students

Some struggling students are also reluctant students. Students who perceive themselves as failures are accustomed to viewing any kind of feedback as confirmation that they are "stupid." Often they don't really hear or use the information contained in the feedback, however well intentioned. For these students, feedback must deal with the negative feelings first and then provide just enough information so that the student has the confidence to understand and use it.

Pay special attention to the tone of feedback for these students. A natural tendency when presented with work that is far off the mark for a learning target is to say just that. That is, the natural tendency is to explain that this is wrong, and that is wrong, and this is poor, and that could be better. Many teachers speak this way to their unsuccessful students, treating them very differently than their successful students (Allington, 2002).

This kind of communication, of course, becomes a self-fulfilling prophecy. Good students get support and improve because of it. Poor students don't hear the information contained in your message because it gets blocked by the overall message of judgment ("This is another pretty bad piece of work I've done"). The issue isn't what you need to say; it's what the student needs to hear. If your feedback comes across like the offstage "Wawh-wawh-wawh" of the teacher in the Charlie Brown cartoons, it isn't feedback; it's noise.

Lying to the student about the quality of work isn't good feedback either. Recall the story in Chapter 3 about the teacher education student who thought it was kind to tell a student he did a good job when he didn't. What should you do if you can't find much good in the work? The strategies suggested for struggling students (see Figure 8.1) offer a way around this conundrum. Focus your feedback on the process the student uses. Use self-referenced feedback. Comment on one or two important points and suggest small steps for improvement. Use simple vocabulary, and check for understanding of content-related terms. Finally, check for understanding of your feedback itself.

Self-referenced feedback compares a student's work with that student's own past performance or with your expectations based on that past performance. If you can describe how this work is better than, or builds on, previous work the student has done, you can say something that is positive—and true. More important for its function as feedback, this kind of comment gives the student information about learning he or she actually did. In the terms of our previous discussion, it positions the student as an agent, and it communicates the fact that you noticed that learning.

I had the opportunity once to do some work in a heterogeneous 3rd grade classroom in a small city. The teacher was very experienced, and her class was well organized. The classroom atmosphere was all about learning, but fun at the same time. The teacher cared deeply about her students, and they knew it. I am sure about this because I interviewed many of them. Her class was a great place to be.

One student in the class was always struggling. He read more slowly than everyone else. He had more trouble with his assignments than everyone else and was usually the last one finished. He often looked puzzled when others seemed to understand. He printed, making big letters, while everyone else wrote in cursive. His writing assignments were usually the shortest in the class. Most of the time he was a surprisingly good sport about all of this, but as the year wore on he seemed to get tired of always being the slowest. Sometimes he would get angry and bang on his chair or desk. More often, he just looked miserable.

However, one assignment was different. The class read a story about a dog, and the theme was that the dog was obedient. The teacher assigned students to write a paragraph titled "Obedience," describing what it meant to them. The purpose of the assignment was for the students to explore the theme of the story and connect it to their own lives and, of course, to develop writing skills. This time, the struggling student had something to say. He covered two pages with better-looking printing than usual. He described the importance of obedience for people. He wrote about how important it is to do what you're told, even when you don't want to. His story seemed to reflect lessons from home. The tone was warm and moving, although there was a hint that he might have disobeyed his parents a time or two to have received the lecture he was passing on in his writing.

I have always believed that the teacher missed an opportunity there to give some really positive feedback. The student did receive a better grade for this paper than he was accustomed to getting, but to my knowledge the teacher didn't make any additional comments. This would have been a wonderful opportunity for some self-referenced feedback, comparing this very nice writing assignment with his previous ones. His sentences were longer and more detailed, and there was more flow. Noticing and naming the characteristics of this piece of writing, and talking with the student about how he had produced it, could have helped him try to reproduce some of these characteristics in future writing. In addition, such a conversation might have affirmed for him that he had done, and therefore could do, a good job. He was accustomed to thinking of himself as a failure, and it wasn't clear to me from his reaction to this assignment that he understood this piece was all that different.

Figure 8.4 shows an example of a poorly done student paragraph for the "Lunchtime" assignment. This student responded to the same prompt as the student in Chapter 2 but with less success. Focus on the process. What did the student do? One thing she *did* do was to answer the question. The response is insufficient, and it contains four sentences punctuated as two, but it describes

Figure 8.4   Unsuccessful "Lunchtime" Paragraph

Writing prompt: Describe what lunchtime is like for you on a school day. Be sure to tell about your lunchtime so that someone who has never had lunch with you on a school day can understand where you have lunch and what lunchtime is like.

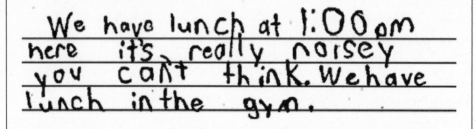

Source: National Assessment of Educational Progress, sample items. Available: http://nces.ed.gov/nationsreportcard/itmrls/

her lunchtime. Appropriate self-referencing would, of course, depend on the specific student's previous work. If the teacher were going to suggest one step for improvement, it would be either to expand the paragraph or to work on the concept of a sentence.

The following dialogue is one example of how the teacher might talk with a student about the poor "Lunchtime" paragraph in Figure 8.4. It assumes that this paragraph was not a good example of the student's work and that usually her paragraphs were better than this. Also, the teacher's evaluation is that the student does understand the concept of a sentence and that the poor mechanics are not the main issue:

Teacher: I read your paragraph. Sounds like you really hate lunchtime. [*This comment is the teacher's honest "reader response" to the paragraph. It shows the student that the teacher heard what she is saying.*]

Student: Yeah.

Teacher: Is that why this paragraph isn't as good as what you usually write? [*This is self-referenced feedback. The teacher notices that the work is not of quality but also communicates that she knows the student has done better.*]

Student: Yeah. I hate lunchtime. I didn't want to write about it.

Teacher: Is the noise the worst part? [*The teacher is going to ask the student to expand the work. The noise seems to be the most salient expression, so it is a logical place to begin the hunt for details.*]

Student: Yeah.

Teacher: Can you tell me about it? [*The teacher invites the student to think about her topic.*]

Student: You can't think. The kids are always yelling, and the teachers yell too.

Teacher: Why is that? [*The teacher is modeling the thought process that should lead to the student identifying details to add.*]

Student: I don't know. When one person yells, you have to yell to be heard over him.

Teacher: OK. Do you think the gym has anything to do with it?

Student: Yeah. The gym is a big room, so there are lots of kids. And everything echoes.

Teacher: You just told me more about the noisy lunchtime than you put in your paragraph. Would you like to rewrite your paragraph to add some of these points to it? [*This comment names for the student the process of identifying details. It offers her a next step that should result in improvement.*]

If the student's revised paragraph is substantially better than the first try, feedback should reflect that. If, for example, details about kids and teachers yelling and sounds echoing were in the new paragraph, the teacher could identify that as a positive step forward. This reluctant student might not, on her own, transfer this small step to more general principles. Therefore, the teacher could point out in the second round of feedback that she had used a process that she could use in other writing. The teacher could describe the process and remind the student what she did: "First you thought about your point, then you went over in your mind what it was that made you think that. It was noisiness in this case, but that process works for writing about other points too. You can use that strategy again."

Feedback for All Students

This chapter showed how to adjust feedback for different types of learners. Successful students benefit from feedback, even though they don't seem to need it as much as some other students. Students who struggle benefit from adjustments to feedback, most noticeably the use of more self-referencing; suggestions of small, doable next steps; and use of a tone that positions the student as someone who can learn, not someone who can't. Adjusting feedback is one part of differentiating instruction and should be used in conjunction with it.

Afterword

Giving effective feedback is a skill that requires practice. Research has identified choices about feedback strategies and content most likely to give students the information they need to improve and the motivation to use it. You should make sure your feedback conforms to these recommendations for content and delivery strategies. Research on formative assessment has found that feedback events need to be episodes of learning for both students and teacher. Teachers should learn something about what students are thinking, and students should learn something about their next steps in learning. Finally, students have to use feedback for it to be effective, and many will not do that independently or spontaneously. You should make sure that feedback is used by building opportunities for students to use feedback into your instruction. We have used the metaphor of three lenses—the lenses in a microscope, a camera, and a telescope—to help you remember to attend to all three of these elements when you give feedback.

Applying this knowledge artfully and effectively in your own classroom requires practice. Most of the examples in this book have been about typical academic subjects and assignments, for maximum readability. However, your particular subject or kind of assignment may not have been represented exactly. Also, each group of students may differ. Every teacher who reads this book should think, "How can I apply these principles and examples to my own classroom?"

In the final analysis, feedback is always adaptive. It always depends on something else. Feedback is based on a learning goal and criteria, a particular assignment, a particular student, and the characteristics of a given piece of work. Feedback also depends on the depth of the teacher's understanding of the topic and of how students learn it.

This book has demonstrated that there are research-based principles upon which to make those adaptations. Good feedback happens when you make sound choices about feedback timing, amount, mode, and audience. Good feedback happens when you focus on the work and the process the student used to do it. Good feedback is criterion-referenced and sometimes self-referenced. Good feedback describes work rather than judges it, is positive, and makes suggestions for improvement. Good feedback is clear and specific. Good feedback helps students become self-regulated learners. Good feedback gives students the help they need to become masters of their own destiny when it comes to learning. Good feedback results in learning for both teacher and student. And finally, feedback is good only if students do learn and become more motivated and your classroom becomes a place where feedback about learning is valued.

Why not select one assignment, class, or activity with which to try some of the suggestions in this book? Observe your students' reactions and reflect on both what you did and how students responded. Move forward to make your feedback even better on the basis of these observations and reflections.

If you are interested in reading more about feedback, lots of information is available. The ASCD Action Tool *Formative Assessment Strategies for Every Classroom* (2nd ed., Brookhart, 2010) includes activities teachers and students can do to give each other feedback about the learning that is taking place. Each activity is accompanied by directions, a description of what to look for in students' comments, and a photocopy master.

For those who would like to read additional professional books for teachers, I can recommend several. Fisher and Frey's *Checking for Understanding* (2007) describes strategies teachers can use to check for student understanding of the concepts and skills that make up their learning targets. Checking for understanding, as this book has demonstrated, is an important part of the formative assessment cycle and essential for understanding how students are processing feedback.

Johnston's *Choice Words: How Our Language Affects Children's Learning* (2004) gives teachers lots of ideas on how to phrase the verbal (written and oral) feedback they give to students. As this book has shown, the content of feedback is critical. How we speak to children matters, and it shapes the way they understand what learning is (Dweck, 2007).

For readers who want shorter, article-length treatments of formative assessment and feedback issues, I recommend Stiggins's "Assessment Through the Student's Eyes" (2007), Dweck's "The Perils and Promises of Praise" (2007), my own "Preventing Feedback Fizzle" (2012), or any of the articles in the December 2007/January 2008 special issue or the September 2012 special issue of *Educational Leadership*. For readers who would like to dip into the scholarly literature on feedback, I recommend Hattie and Timperley's (2007) review, "The Power of Feedback." It is a comprehensive and quite readable summary of the literature on feedback.

References

Allal, L. (2011). Pedagogy, didactics and the co-regulation of learning: A perspective from the French-language world of educational research. *Research Papers in Education, 26*(3), 329–336.

Allington, R. L. (2002). What I've learned about effective reading instruction from a decade of studying exemplary elementary classroom teachers. *Phi Delta Kappan, 83*(10), 740–747.

Andrade, H., & Brookhart, S. M. (in press). The role of classroom assessment in supporting self-regulated learning.

Andrade, H. L., & Brown, G. T. L., (in press). Student self-assessment in the classroom. In G. T. L. Brown and L. Harris, (Eds.). *Handbook of Human and Social Conditions in Assessment*. London: Routledge.

Andrade, H., & Valtcheva, A. (2009). Promoting learning and achievement through self-assessment. *Theory into Practice, 48*(1), 12–19.

Arter, J., & McTighe, J. (2001). *Scoring rubrics in the classroom*. Thousand Oaks, CA: Corwin Press.

Bangert-Drowns, R. L., Kulik, C. C., Kulik, J. A., & Morgan, M. (1991). The instructional effect of feedback in test-like events. *Review of Educational Research, 61*(2), 213–238.

Brookhart, S. M. (2001). Successful students' formative and summative use of assessment information. *Assessment in Education, 8*(2), 153–169.

Brookhart, S. M. (2010). *Formative assessment strategies for every classroom* (2nd ed.). Alexandria, VA: ASCD.

Brookhart, S. M. (2013). *How to create and use rubrics for formative assessment and grading*. Alexandria, VA: ASCD.

Brown, G. T. L., & Harris, L. R. (2013). Student self-assessment. In. J. H. McMillan (Ed.), *Sage handbook of research on classroom assessment* (pp. 367–393). Los Angeles: Sage.

Butler, D. L., Schnellert, L., & Perry, N. E. (in press). *Developing self-regulating learners*. Don Mills, ON: Pearson.

Butler, D. L., & Winne, P. H. (1995). Feedback and self-regulated learning: A theoretical synthesis. *Review of Educational Research, 65*(3), 245–281.

Butler, R., & Nisan, M. (1986). Effects of no feedback, task-related comments, and grades on intrinsic motivation and performance. *Journal of Educational Psychology, 78*(3), 210–216.

Dalton, S. S. (1998). *Pedagogy matters: Standards for effective teaching practice*. Research Report No. 4, Center for Research on Education, Diversity, and Excellence, University of California, Santa Cruz. Available: http://www.cal.org/crede/pubs/research/RR4.pdf

Dweck, C. S. (2007). The perils and promises of praise. *Educational Leadership, 65*(2), 34–39.

Fisher, D., & Frey, N. (2007). *Checking for understanding*. Alexandria, VA: ASCD.

Gamlem, S. M., & Smith, K. (2013). Student perceptions of classroom feedback. *Assessment in Education, 20*(2), 150–169.

Hattie, J. A. C. (2009). *Visible learning: A synthesis of over 800 meta-analyses relating to achievement*. London: Routledge.

Hattie, J., & Timperley, H. (2007). The power of feedback. *Review of Educational Research, 77*(1), 81–112.

Heritage, M., Kim, J., Vendlinski, T., & Herman, J. (2009). From evidence to action: A seamless process in formative assessment? *Educational Measurement: Issues and Practice, 28*(3), 24–31.

Hill, J. D., & Flynn, K. M. (2006). *Classroom instruction that works with English language learners*. Alexandria, VA: ASCD.

Johnston, P. H. (2004). *Choice words: How our language affects children's learning*. Portland, ME: Stenhouse.

Kluger, A. N., & DeNisi, A. (1996). The effects of feedback interventions on performance: A historical review, a meta-analysis, and a preliminary feedback intervention theory. *Psychological Bulletin, 119*(2), 254–284.

Kroog, H. I., Ruiz-Primo, M. A., & Sands, D. (2014). *Understanding the interplay between the cultural context of classrooms and formative assessment*. Paper presented at the annual meeting of the American Educational Research Association, Philadelphia.

Lazarus, S., & Brookhart, S. M. (2016). *Formative assessment for students with disabilities*. Washington, DC: Council of Chief State School Officers.

Mason, B. J., & Bruning, R. (2001). *Providing feedback in computer-based instruction: What the research tells us*. University of Nebraska-Lincoln. Available: http://dwb.unl.edu/Edit/MB/MasonBruning.html

Minstrell, J., Anderson, R., & Li, M. (2009). *Assessing teacher competency in formative assessment*. Annual Report to the National Science Foundation.

Mo, W. (2007). "Can you listen faster?" Assessment of students who are culturally and linguistically diverse learners. In P. Jones, J. F. Carr, & R. L. Ataya (Eds.), *A pig don't get fatter the more you weigh it: Classroom assessments that work* (pp. 39–50). New York: Teachers College Press.

Moss, C. M., & Brookhart, S. M. (2009). *Advancing formative assessment in every classroom: A guide for instructional leaders*. Alexandria, VA: ASCD.

Moss, C. M., & Brookhart, S. M. (2012). *Learning targets: Helping students aim for understanding in today's lesson*. Alexandria, VA: ASCD.

Moss, C. M., & Brookhart, S. M. (2015). *Formative classroom walkthroughs: How principals and teachers collaborate to raise student achievement*. Alexandria, VA: ASCD.

Nicol, D. J., & Macfarlane-Dick, D. (2006). Formative assessment and self-regulated learning: A model and seven principles of good feedback practice. *Studies in Higher Education, 31*(2), 199–218.

Page, E. B. (1958). Teacher comments and student performance: A seventy-four classroom experiment in school motivation. *Journal of Educational Psychology, 49*(4), 173–181.

Panadero, E. (2016). Social, interpersonal, and human effects of peer assessment: A review and future directions. In G. T. L. Brown and L. Harris, (Eds.). *Handbook of Human and Social Conditions in Assessment*. London: Routledge.

Pintrich, P., & Zusho, A. (2002). The development of academic self-regulation: The role of cognitive and motivational factors. In J. Eccles, & A. Wigfield (Eds.), *Development of achievement motivation* (pp. 249–284). San Diego, CA: Academic Press.

Reed, B., & Railsback, J. (2003, May). *Strategies and resources for mainstream teachers of English language learners*. Portland, OR: Northwest Regional Educational Laboratory.

Ross, J. A. (2006). The reliability, validity, and utility of self-assessment. *Practical Assessment Research and Evaluation, 11*(10). Retrieved from http://pareonline.net/getvn.asp?v=11&n=10

Sadler, D. R. (1989). Formative assessment and the design of instructional systems. *Instructional Science, 18*(2), 119–144.

Sadler, P. M., & Good, E. (2006). The impact of self- and peer-grading on student learning. *Educational Assessment, 11*(1), 1–31.

Shute, V. J. (2008). Focus on formative feedback. *Review of Educational Research, 78*(1), 153–189.

Stewart, L. G., & White, M. A. (1976). Teacher comments, letter grades, and student performance: What do we really know? *Journal of Educational Psychology, 68*(4), 488–500.

Stiggins, R. J. (2007). Assessment through the student's eyes. *Educational Leadership, 64*(8), 22–26.

Thorndike, E. L. (1913). *Educational psychology. Volume I: The original nature of man*. New York: Columbia University, Teachers College.

Topping, K. J. (2013). Peers as a source of formative and summative assessment. In. J. H. McMillan (Ed.), *Sage handbook of research on classroom assessment* (pp. 395–412). Los Angeles: Sage.

Tunstall, P., & Gipps, C. (1996). Teacher feedback to young children in formative assessment: A typology. *British Educational Research Journal, 22*(4), 389–404.

van der Kleij, F. M., Feskens, R. C. W., & Eggen T. J. H. M. (2015). Effects of feedback in a computer-based learning environment on student outcomes: A meta-analysis. *Review of Educational Research, 85*(4), 475–511.

Wiliam, D. (2011). *Embedded formative assessment*. Bloomington, IN: Solution Tree.

Zimmerman, B., & Schunk, D. (Eds.). (2011). *Handbook of self-regulation of learning and performances*. New York: Routledge.

Index

About the Author

Susan M. Brookhart is an independent educational consultant and author based in Helena, Montana. She currently serves as an adjunct faculty member in the School of Education at Duquesne University. She was the 2007–2009 editor of *Educational Measurement: Issues and Practice*, a journal of the National Council on Measurement in Education, and she is currently an Associate Editor of *Applied Measurement in Education*. She is author or coauthor of 17 books and more than 70 articles and book chapters on classroom assessment, teacher professional development, and evaluation. She was named the 2014 Jason Millman Scholar by the Consortium for Research on Educational Assessment and Teaching Effectiveness (CREATE) and is the recipient of the 2015 Samuel J. Messick Memorial Lecture Award from ETS/TOEFL. Dr. Brookhart's interests include the role of both formative and summative classroom assessment in student motivation and achievement, the connection between classroom assessment and large-scale assessment, and grading. She works with schools, districts, regional educational service units, and universities doing professional development and consultation. She may be reached at susanbrookhart@bresnan.net.

Related Resources

At the time of publication, the following ASCD resources were available (ASCD stock numbers appear in parentheses). For up-to-date information about ASCD resources, go to www.ascd.org. You can search the complete archives of *Educational Leadership* at http://www.ascd.org/el.

Print Products

Educational Leadership: Looking at Student Work (April 2016) (#116034)

Educational Leadership: Questioning for Learning (September 2015) (#116028)

Educational Leadership: Instruction that Sticks (October 2014) (#115017)

Educational Leadership: Using Assessments Thoughtfully (March 2014) (#114023)

Educational Leadership: Feedback for Learning (September 2012) (#113032)

Educational Leadership: Effective Grading Practices (November 2011) (#112018)

Learning in the Fast Lane: 8 Ways to Put ALL Students on the Road to Academic Success by Suzy Pepper Rollins (#114026)

Exploring Formative Assessment (The Professional Learning Community Series) by Susan M. Brookhart (#109038)

How to Assess Higher-Order Thinking Skills in Your Classroom by Susan M. Brookhart (#109111)

Advancing Formative Assessment in Every Classroom: A Guide for Instructional Leaders by Connie M. Moss and Susan M. Brookhart (#109031)

Becoming a Great High School: 6 Strategies and 1 Attitude That Make a Difference by Tim R. Westerberg (#109052)

Formative Assessment Strategies for Every Classroom, 2nd Edition by Susan M. Brookhart (#111005)

How to Design Questions and Tasks to Assess Student Thinking by Susan M. Brookhart (#114014)

Learning Targets: Helping Students Aim for Understanding in Today's Lesson by Connie M. Moss and Susan M. Brookhart (#112002)

How to Make Decisions with Different Kinds of Student Assessment Data by Susan M. Brookhart (#116003)

Read, Write, Lead: Breakthrough Strategies for Schoolwide Literacy Success by Regie Routman (#113016)

Formative Classroom Walkthroughs: How Principals and Teachers Collaborate to Raise Student Achievement by Connie M. Moss and Susan M. Brookhart (#115003)

How to Create and Use Rubrics for Formative Assessment and Grading by Susan M. Brookhart (#112001)

What Works in Schools: Translating Research into Action by Robert J. Marzano (#102271)

For more information, send e-mail to member@ascd.org; call 1-800-933-2723 or 703-578-9600, press 2; send a fax to 703-575-5400; or write to Information Services, ASCD, 1703 N. Beauregard St., Alexandria, VA 22311-1714 USA.

BLAME YOUR PARENTS

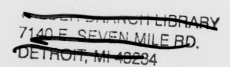
Buffy Silverman

Raintree

Chicago, Illinois

an imprint of Capstone Global Library, LLC
Chicago, Illinois

Customer Service 888-454-2279

Visit our website at www.heinemannraintree.com

Designed by Philippa Jenkins and Q2A Creative

Printed in the United States of America, North Mankato, Minnesota.

13 12 11
10 9 8 7 6 5

Library of Congress Cataloging-in-Publication Data
Silverman, Buffy
  Blame your parents / Buffy Silverman.
     p. cm.
  Includes bibliographical references and index.
  ISBN-13: 978-1-4109-2841-2 (library binding)
  ISBN-10: 1-4109-2841-1 (library binding)
  ISBN-13: 978-1-4109-2858-0 (pbk.)
  ISBN-10: 1-4109-2858-6 (pbk.)
 1. Human genetics--Juvenile literature.
 I. Title.
  QH437.5.S568 2007
  576.5--dc22

                              2006102048

062011
006187RP

Acknowledgments
The author and publisher are grateful to the following for permission to reproduce copyright material: Alamy p.**16** (Danita Delimont); Corbis pp.**18-19** (Annie Engel/zefa), **7** (Ralph A. Clevenger), **24** (Royalty-Free), **4-5** (Tom and Dee Ann McCarthy), **23** (Tom Stewart/zefa); FLPA p.**25** (David Hosking), **27** (Nigel Cattlin); NHPA pp.**8-9** (Stephen Dalton); Photolibrary.com p.**21** (Animals Animals/Earth Scenes), **14** (Botanica), **20** (Phototake Inc), **6** (Wendy Shattil & Bob Rozinski/Oxford Scientific), **12-13** (Workbook, Inc); Science Photo Library pp.**10-11** (Prof. K.Seddon and Dr. T.Evans, Queen's University Belfast).

Cover photograph of various images to form a counterfit face reproduced with permission of Corbis (Lucidio Studio Inc, Serge Krouglikoff); photos.com.

Illustrations by Peter Geissler.

The publishers would like to thank Nancy Harris and Harold Pratt for their assistance in the preparation of this book.

Every effort has been made to contact copyright holders of any material reproduced in this book. Any omissions will be rectified in subsequent printings if notice is given to the publishers.